More snapper in the bay

Want more snapper in the bay? It'll soon be a reality, as we meet a commitment to remove commercial netting from Port Phillip.

The last nets will leave the bay in 2021, and there'll be more of the bay's key species for recreational fishers just like you.

It's a key commitment in the government's *Target One Million* Plan to make fishing even better and means there'll be more of the bay's bread and butter species for you to enjoy with family and friends.

Your fishing licence fees at work

VICTORIA
State Government

Authorised by the Victorian Government, 1 Treasury Place, Melbourne

LANDBASED FISHING GUIDE
PORT PHILLIP BAY

LANDBASED FISHING GUIDE

PORT PHILLIP BAY

ALL THE TOP LANDBASED FISHING LOCATIONS

JUSTIN FELIX

First published 2013
Reprinted 2015
Reprinted 2021

Published and distributed by
AFN Fishing & Outdoors
PO Box 544 Croydon, Victoria 3136
Telephone: (03) 9729 8788 Facsimile: (03) 9729 7833
Email: sales@afn.com.au
Website: www.afn.com.au

©Australian Fishing Network 2013

ISBN: 9781 8651 3230 3

CONTENTS

DEDICATION

This book is dedicated to my grandfather who would be proud of my efforts.

Thank you to my parents for ensuring his lessons were never lost on me.

To my partner Kristyna – I don't know how you put up with me fishing all the time but I'm grateful for your patience and for not busting my chops about it. You're one of a kind and I love you for it!

To all my fishing buddies who spend countless hours with me on the piers, beaches and rockwalls of Port Phillip Bay – I'm glad I've instilled the fishing bug in you all.

By Nigel Webster

Shorebased platforms provide the foundation from which so many of us start our fishing journeys. I have been fishing shorebased locations around Australia and parts of Africa for the past 16 years. Today with two children in tow, I once again spend much of my time exploring the joys of catching fish from shore. There is a unique sense of ease and pleasure which can be found when fishing from shore; although there are boats and kayaks in my garage I still love the simplicity of grabbing a few rods, a tackle box, some bait or lures and heading to the nearest shoreline. It provides me with a sense of amusement that many of us, I included, spend a great deal of money on boats and then once on the water, spend much of our time casting towards shore. This suggests that there is a distinct advantage in fishing from shore, and that with a little guidance and good technique, the shorebased 'fisho' stands to catch some memorable fish.

I met Justin Felix several years ago when he arrived at the Australian Fishing Network (AFN) offices and took on the role of Managing Editor. Justin has spent most of his time fishing and writing about the shorebased fishing around Port Phillip Bay. He is passionate about and has an intimate fishing knowledge of this part of the world: I can think of no-one better to guide you through how to best take advantage of fishing our key local shorebased spots.

Shorebased fishing, in certain situations, is recognised as being one of the more dangerous activities we Australians partake in. The combination of weather and water has the potential to become deadly in short time. We at AFN encourage anglers of all persuasions to get outdoors and make the most of this great country we have, but take your common sense with you. Many disasters within the angling fraternity could have been averted by simply avoiding potentially dangerous weather and water conditions. Please take heed of safety warnings, alerts and signage and when in the company of young and inexperienced anglers, supervise and take extra care with them. In the event that there is the potential for you or your children to end up in the water, consider the use of lifejackets and suitable clothing.

Enjoying the outdoors means exposure to the elements and this bears a certain level of risk. Our sun is a silent killer and Australians need to protect themselves from it. Every fishing trip should include planning that includes sun protection for you and your family. Hats, 50 plus sunscreen, zinc, full length clothing and good water supplies should all be first packed when heading outdoors.

Disclaimer
General
Every effort has been made to ensure that the nature of fishing locations listed in this book have been adequately described using current access arrangements, quality of available fishing platform, facilities and other public user information. However, we cannot guarantee that changes won't occur. In the event that circumstances change, AFN take no responsibility for trespass, changes to infrastructure, responsibility for injuries incurred and incident sustained while accessing locations described in this book.   All areas detailed in this book must be accessed with due care to personal safety, environment and local property.

Marine Park
Many parts of our coastline encompass areas of Marine Park these days. Various zoning arrangements exist within areas of Marine Park. Specific zoning regulations may dictate that recreational anglers are not permitted to fish within certain areas. If you plan to fish recreationally, it is recommended that familiarity with prohibited fishing areas is gained. AFN have made every effort to identify locations where recreational fishing is prohibited, however, these requirements may change in future times. It is the responsibility of anglers to fish within the legal requirements as stipulated by the Victorian Government.

Fish Identification & Regulations
This publication provides an interpretation of data pertaining to various Victorian fish species, and regulated bag and size limits. These regulations may change following printing of this publication. It is every angler's responsibility to stay abreast of current fishing regulation changes. AFN take no responsibility for misinterpretation of government data, legislative changes following printing of this publication and reporting of illegal catches to relevant authorities. Further reference to current Victorian fishing regulations can be found at www.dpi.vic.gov.au.

Like many keen anglers, fishing for me started at a very young age. My grandfather taught me the basic principles of bait fishing and we'd always manage a good feed of silver trevally from Sawtells Inlet in Tooradin. While I wasn't fortunate enough to fish with him 'til an age that I can clearly remember, I'm forever grateful for the fishing bug he instilled in me.

My dad took the reigns soon after my grandfather passed and I fondly recall chasing squid and leatherjacket from the various piers along the Mornington Peninsula. Funnily enough this is still a great passion of mine and I can be found along the Peninsula on a weekly basis. There's just something special about chasing our piscatorial delights with two feet planted firmly on the ground.

There's no denying – landbased fishing can be frustrating at times but I think that's what adds so much to its appeal. Every session is a challenge and if you do go home empty handed, don't give up, take it as a lesson learned instead. Port Phillip Bay is a vast expanse of water that provides plenty of options for the landbased angler so get out there and start exploring.

Justin Felix

1. PORTSEA PIER
2. SORRENTO BOAT RAMP PIER
3. SORRENTO PIER
4. COUTA BAY SAILING CLUB JETTY
5. BLAIRGOWRIE PIER
6. RYE PIER
7. ROSEBUD PIER
8. McCRAE ROCK WALL
9. DROMANA PIER
10. SAFETY BEACH BOAT RAMP JETTY
11. MARTHA COVE BEACH
12. MT MARTHA CLIFFS
13. BALCOMBE CREEK BEACH
14. FISHERMAN'S BEACH BOAT RAMP
15. MORNINGTON PIER
16. CANADIAN BAY
17. DAVEYS BAY
18. OLIVERS HILL
19. FRANKSTON PIER
20. SEAFORD PIER
21. PATTERSON RIVER
22. CHELSEA BEACH
23. MORDIALLOC PIER
24. PARKDALE BEACH
25. BEAUMARIS YACHT SQUADRON JETTY
26. HALF MOON BAY JETTY
27. HALF MOON BAY ROCKS
28. SANDRINGHAM BREAKWALL
29. HAMPTON ROCK GROYNES
30. BRIGHTON BEACH
31. BRIGHTON BEACH BREAKWATER
32. ST KILDA PIER
33. KERFERD ROAD PIER
34. LAGOON PIER
35. SANDRIDGE BEACH ROCK GROYNES
36. THE WARMIES
37. FERGUSON STREET PIER
38. WILLIAMSTOWN BEACH ROCKWALL
39. ALTONA PIER
40. WERRIBEE RIVER
41. GRAMMAR SCHOOL LAGOON
42. NORTH SHORE ROCKS
43. MORPANYAL PARK BEACH
44. ST HELENS ROCKWALL
45. GRIFFIN GULLY JETTY

46. LIMEBURNERS POINT BREAKWALL
47. CUNNINGHAM PIER
48. GEELONG WATERFRONT
49. PORTARLINGTON JETTY
50. ST LEONARDS PIER
51. SWAN BAY JETTY
52. LAKERS CUTTING
53. QUEENSCLIFF PIER
54. THE CUT – QUEENSCLIFF
55. POINT LONSDALE PIER

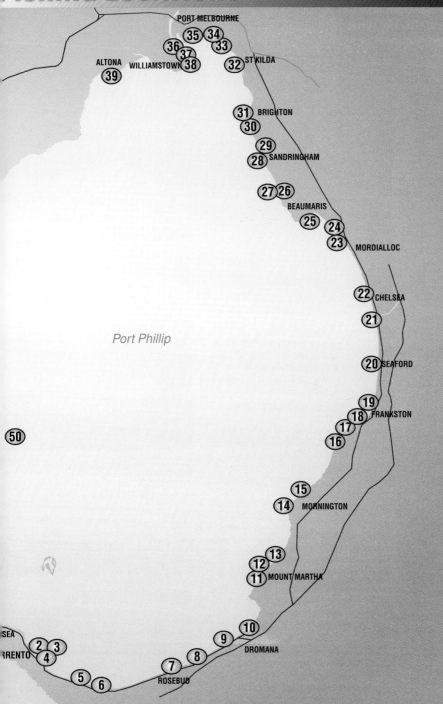

Port Phillip

PORTSEA PIER

Point Nepean Road, Portsea. Follow Point Nepean Road past Sorrento until you see the Portsea Pub on the right hand side. The pier is serviced by a car park across the road but be mindful of parking limits during summer.

🔍 SNAPSHOT

PLATFORM
PIER

TARGET SPECIES
SQUID
CUTTLEFISH
KING GEORGE WHITING
SALMON
TREVALLY
FLATHEAD
CUTTLEFISH
TOMMY ROUGH
GARFISH

BEST BAITS
FRESH SQUID, PIPI, SILVERFISH, MAGGOTS, MUSSELS, SILVER WHITING

BEST LURES
ARTIFICIAL SQUID JIGS, SOFT PLASTIC WORMS AND GRUBS

BEST TIMES
TIDE CHANGE AROUND DAWN OR DUSK

SEASONS

Squid
Year round/Spring for the big models

King George whiting
Summer months

Australian salmon
Winter

Garfish
Year round but best in winter

Flathead
Summer

Others
Year round

Portsea Pier is one of, if not the most consistent producers of squid in Port Phillip Bay. The pier is surrounded by vast amounts of weed beds that attract a wide variety of species and anglers alike. While many fish species can be targeted here it's the cephalopods that receive the most attention.

TACTICS

For your best chance at getting amongst some squid stay mobile and cover as much ground as you can. Work your way along the length of the pier and target areas where weed beds visibly cover the sea floor. For King George whiting cast from the end of the pier with fresh squid and pipi baits on a paternoster rig. Tie your rig from 15 lb leader with two dropper loops that are attached to size 6 long shank hooks. Garfish are best attracted with a fine berley mix that can be made up of weet bix and tuna oil. A good time to fish for them is when the locals are onto it. A size 12 hook suspended under a quill float will produce the best results.

BAITS AND LURES

Squid are best targeted with artificial squid jigs presented in and around the visible weed beds that line the sea floor; however, a silver whiting under a float can often tempt the bigger models. King George whiting are privy to fresh squid, mussel and pipi as are the majority of other species available. Garfish and tommy rough are best targeted with maggots or silverfish under a float while flathead are commonly caught on soft plastics bounced on the bottom.

BEST TIDE/TIMES

Fishing a tide change around dawn or dusk is best for most of the species of offer here. If fishing for squid cast towards the eastern side of the pier during a run in tide and to the western side during a run out tide.

AMENITIES

Public toilets, a playground and BBQ area are all located at the start of the pier as is a set of shops right next to the Portsea Pub.

KIDS AND FAMILIES

A great spot to take the kids and family for the day thanks to a range of amenities and plenty of fish on offer to keep the kids entertained.

FINALLY

The pier is a year round fishery thanks to its close proximity to Port Phillip Heads and the fact that it's surrounded by weed beds that provide plenty of food and habitat for marine species.

SORRENTO BOAT RAMP JETTY

HOW TO GET THERE

St Aubins Way, Sorrento. Take Point Nepean Road past the Sorrento ferry pier and turn right into St Aubins Way. Follow the road around the car park until you reach the boat ramp.

SNAPSHOT

PLATFORM
JETTY

TARGET SPECIES
SQUID
GARFISH
TOMMY ROUGH
KING GEORGE WHITING
SNOOK
SILVER TREVALLY

BEST BAITS
SQUID STRIPS, PIPI, MUSSEL, SILVER WHITING

BEST LURES
SQUID JIGS, SABIKI RIG, SOFT PLASTIC CURL TAIL WORMS

BEST TIMES
HIGH TIDE DURING LOW-LIGHT LEVELS

This little gem is located at the base of the car park that services the Sorrento Boat Ramp. While not the most popular landbased location in the Mornington Peninsula; the reefy bottom attracts a wide variety of species particularly after dark.

TACTICS

Soft plastic or egi rods in the 1 to 3 or 2 to 4 kg range are the only rods required here. For your best shot at arrive after dark and fan your casts from left to right, starting from over the boat ramp between the two jetties and eventually out towards the Sorrento pier. Work your jigs quickly and don't allow them to sink too long as there are some unforgiving snags here. If the jetty light is on you should be able to see the bottom clearly and snook and trevally can all be seen working the area at various times. Use creature style plastics as well as grubs to try and tempt these fussy feeders. Berley and quill float rigs are best suited to garfish and tommy rough. For King George whiting fish from the rockwall that protects the boat ramp from inclement weather conditions. A paternoster rig tied from a 12 lb leader will suffice.

BAITS AND LURES

Garfish and tommy rough are ideal targets with silver fish and maggots fished under a float rig. For King George whiting try pipi, mussel or fresh squid. The squid in the area are very responsive to artificial jigs but can be targeted with a silver whiting under a float. For all other species try small soft plastics such as grubs or wriggles in 2 to 3 inch models.

BEST TIDE/TIMES

A high tide, particularly after dark, sees a range of species enter the area to feed on the local weed beds and jetty pylons.

AMENITIES

There are no amenities in the immediate area; however, Sorrento park is located up the hill behind the ramp.

KIDS AND FAMILIES

Not the best place for kids as it is a night time proposition only and there isn't much else for them to do here.

FINALLY

An out-of-the-norm landbased location that often gets overlooked because of its size and location. Fish the right times here and you could be pleasantly surprised.

SEASONS

Squid
Summer

Garfish
Year round

Tommy rough
Summer and autumn

King George whiting
November to April

Snook
Summer

Silver trevally
November

SORRENTO PIER

HOW TO GET THERE

Esplanade, Sorrento.
Follow Point Nepean
Road towards Sorrento
before veering right
onto Esplanade at the
ferry terminal pier.

SNAPSHOT

PLATFORM
PIER

TARGET SPECIES
KING GEORGE WHITING
SILVER TREVALLY
SQUID
CUTTLEFISH
FLATHEAD
LEATHERJACKET
WRASSE
AUSTRALIAN SALMON
GARFISH
SLIMY MACKEREL

BEST BAITS
BLUEBAIT, WHITEBAIT,
PIPI, MUSSEL, SQUID,
PILCHARD, SILVER FISH

BEST LURES
SOFT PLASTICS, VIBES,
SQUID JIGS, SABIKI
RIGS.

BEST TIMES
INCOMING TIDE AT
DAWN OR DUSK

SEASONS
King George whiting
November to April

Silver trevally
Spring

Squid
Year round

Garfish
Winter

Flathead
Summer

Other species
Year round

Sorrento pier not only provides a great fishing platform but also the terminal for the ferry that runs between here and Queenscliff. To facilitate the large ferry vessels the pier is surrounded by a deep channel that not only causes the current to rip through but also some great fishing opportunities.

TACTICS

The current rips through here, particular during tide changes thus extra lead may be required for offerings to reach the bottom. Use squid jigs on a paternoster rig to ensure they reach the bottom otherwise a quick sinking jig or something in the 3.0 to 3.5 size will suffice. Target the weed beds on the left hand side of the jetty for your best shot at King George whiting, especially after dark on a high tide. A paternoster rig tied from 10 or 12 lb leader will be adequate along with a 2 oz bomb sinker. Flathead and Australian salmon can be caught with soft plastics cast around the deeper water. For your best shot at wrasse and leatherjacket cast baits around the ferry pylons particularly as the ferry is coming or going.

BAITS AND LURES

Squid are best targeted on squid jigs but can also be caught with silver whiting under a float if the current isn't ripping through. If you can catch a squid use some of it for King George whiting as they find it hard to resist freshly caught bait. Silver trevally respond well to both sabiki jigs and creature style soft plastics around the pylons whereas garfish and slimy mackerel can be caught on silver fish and pilchard slithers.

BEST TIDE/TIMES

The squid fishing really picks up after dark here and is usually highlighted by the locals that can be seen targeting them on a regular basis under the lights. Incoming tides also seem to fish better than outgoing tides here.

AMENITIES

The car park is big so plenty of car spots are available. Public toilets, cafés and a playground are all in close proximity too.

KIDS AND FAMILIES

The pier is wide however the main fishing platform lacks in railings so kids must be supervised at all times. Shelter exists is it does happen to rain though.

FINALLY

A very productive location that is generally quieter than nearby Portsea and Blairgowrie piers, making it a great option during summer.

COUTA BAY SAILING CLUB JETTY

HOW TO GET THERE

Point Nepean Road, Sorrento. Take Point Nepean Road towards Sorrento and turn right into the Sailing Clubs car park which is marked by flag poles before Holyrood Avenue.

SNAPSHOT

PLATFORM
PIER

TARGET SPECIES
KING GEORGE WHITING
SQUID
PINKIE SNAPPER
SILVER TREVALLY
GARFISH

BEST BAITS
SQUID, MUSSEL, PIPI, PILCHARDS, BLUEBAIT, SILVER FISH, MAGGOTS, SILVER WHITING

BEST LURES
SQUID JIGS, SOFT PLASTIC WORMS

BEST TIMES
INCOMING TIDE

This jetty is one that is often overlooked as it can appear to be private property to the naked eye. The narrow structure covers a shallow sandy bottom until the end where it opens up amongst boat moorings and a reefy bottom. This is where all of the action takes place.

TACTICS

The weed beds that are interspersed throughout the boat moorings provide the perfect habitat for the species that inhabit this area. King George whiting can be targeted here with 7 to 9 ft rods with 1 or 2 oz bomb sinkers. Both paternoster and running sinker rigs will work here so long as they are tied from a fluorocarbon leader in the 8 to 10 lb range. Squid can be targeted with 2.5 to 3.0 size squid jigs and if there aren't too many people around you can tempt them with a baited jig left out under a float. Pinkie snapper can also be targeted amongst the boat moorings with either soft plastics or bluebait on a 2/0 baitholder hook. Garfish can be caught in big numbers here provided conditions are calm and a suitable amount of berley is used to attract them to the area. Fish either the incoming or outgoing tide for best results here.

BAITS AND LURES

Squid jigs are suitable for the squid here, as are whole fish baits such as silver whiting or pilchards rigged on a squid prong under a float. King George whiting are privy to mussel, squid and pipi while pinkie snapper are best targeted with half pillies, bluebait and squid strips. Silver trevally can be caught whilst targeting garfish on float rigs but are best fished for with creature style soft plastics such as the Damiki Monter Miki or the Berkley PowerBait Micro Power Nymphs.

BEST TIDE/TIMES

Incoming or outgoing tides during dawn or dusk and into the night will see most fish species caught; however this is a location where fish can be caught all throughout the day.

AMENITIES

There are no public amenities in the area so be prepared if you plan to spend a few hours here. A restaurant is located within the sailing club for lunch and dinner.

KIDS AND FAMILIES

The jetty is narrow without railings on the main fishing platform so kids must be supervised at all times here. The surrounding beach offers shallow water perfect for swimming if the fishing is quiet.

FINALLY

A popular location for locals and for good reason too. A wide variety of species can effectively be targeted from this narrow platform if the right tactics are employed.

SEASONS

King George whiting
November to April

Squid
Year round

Pinkie snapper
Summer and Autumn

Silver trevally
Spring

Garfish
Winter and spring

BLAIRGOWRIE PIER

🔍 HOW TO GET THERE

Point Nepean Road, Blairgowrie. Follow Point Nepean Road south along the coast past Blairgowrie Village on the left. Veer right down the ramp where the Blairgowrie Yacht Squadron sign is located. This ramp takes you directly down to beach level although another car park exists on Point Nepean Road where a set of stairs will take you down to the beach.

🔍 SNAPSHOT

PLATFORM
PIER

TARGET SPECIES
SQUID, KING GEORGE WHITING, FLATHEAD, AUSTRALIAN SALMON, GARFISH, YAKKAS, SILVER TREVALLY

BEST BAITS
SILVERFISH, MAGGOTS, SQUID, MUSSEL, BLUEBAIT, PIPI

BEST LURES
SOFT PLASTICS, BLADES, METAL SLUGS

BEST TIMES
TIDE CHANGE AROUND DAWN OR DUSK

SEASONS

Squid
Year round

King George whiting
Spring and summer

Garfish
Year round

Flathead
Summer months

Others
Year round

Blairgowrie Pier has become one of the most popular and consistent piers along the Mornington Peninsula in recent years. Its sturdy construction and plenty of abounding structure makes it a real fish attractor. The bottom consists of a mainly sandy bottom with plenty of weed interspersed.

TACTICS

It is worth bringing two or three outfits here as you never know what might turn up. A soft plastic rod in the 2 to 4 kg range is ideal for casting soft plastics, squid jigs and metal lures around. A 7 ft nibble tip rod is perfect for gars and King George whiting and a light surf rod can be handy for throwing baits a long distance in search of the local flathead population. Berley is effective here, especially for garfish and salmon and once you've attracted them to your immediate area it can be a fish a cast. When fishing after dark, focus most of your attention under the lights as this is where most of the squid are caught and always cast a few soft plastics around the start of the pier as flathead can often be found there. King George whiting are best targeted along the final third of the pier where plenty of weed patches exist.

BAITS AND LURES

If garfish are your target don't leave home without silverfish and maggots. Send them out under a pencil float after you have berleyed the area. King George whiting can be caught with fresh squid and pipi and flathead respond well to bluebait, soft plastics and blade lures. The local salmon population can turn up in droves and when they do it's time to pull out the metal lures and soft plastic stickbaits.

BEST TIDE/TIMES

Early mornings and late afternoons are most productive here but some exceptional squid fishing can also be had after dark. Focus most of your attention on an incoming or outgoing tide and watch what the locals are doing.

AMENITIES

Apart from good car parks and a sandy beach there aren't any amenities in the immediate area.

KIDS AND FAMILIES

A good sturdy platform to take the kids for the day with especially because of the clear water that they can see plenty of marine life through.

FINALLY

Blairgowrie has cemented its place as one of the most productive landbased locations in the Mornington Peninsula and for good reason too – it really is that good.

HOW TO GET THERE

Point Nepean Road, Rye. Follow Point Nepean Road into Rye and look for the big car park opposite the strip of shops in the heart of town.

SNAPSHOT

PLATFORM
PIER

TARGET SPECIES
SQUID
FLATHEAD
KING GEORGE
 WHITING
PINKIE SNAPPER
GARFISH
TOMMY ROUGH
BRONZE WHALER
SHARKS

BEST BAITS
SQUID, PIPI,
BLUEBAIT, MUSSEL,
PIPI, SILVER FISH,
MAGGOTS,
WHOLE SALMON,
TUNA FILLET

BEST LURES
SQUID JIGS, SOFT
PLASTIC GRUBS AND
WORMS

BEST TIMES
HIGH TIDE AT DAWN
OR DUSK

SEASONS

Squid
Spring and summer

Flathead
Summer

King George whitin
December to March

Pinkie snapper
Autumn

Garfish
Winter

Tommy rough
Year round

Bronze whaler sharks
Summer

R ye Pier is one of the busiest landbased locations during the holiday season due to its proximity to popular shops and its ability to produce an array of species.

TACTICS

Squid are best targeted under the lights here after dark so try to get a spot before the sun hits the horizon. Casting squid jigs in sizes 2.5 and 3.0 will yield the best results. Flathead can be caught on soft plastics especially near the sandbar that runs the length of Rye beach. Garfish are prolific towards the end of the pier during winter and are best targeted with plenty of berley and a float rig. Tommy rough and mackerel will often be caught with the same technique. If you want to target a bronze whaler do so in December and balloon a big bait off the end of the pier during an offshore blow. Be prepared though as the sharks encountered can be quite large. Game outfits are the norm for this style of fishing as anything less will have you shaking in your boots.

BAITS AND LURES

For the bronzies try using a whole salmon or small bonito under a balloon. Garfish and tommy rough will bite best on silver fish and maggots under a float rig. Squid can be caught with a baited skewer but are best targeted here with a squid jig. Squid, pipi and mussel will undo the King George whiting here whilst flathead respond best to soft plastics cast around the sand flats.

BEST TIDE/TIMES

The water is shallow here until the last quarter of the pier where it drops off into 2 or 3 m so fish an incoming tide for best results.

AMENITIES

A large car park services the pier as well as a long strip of shops that sit directly opposite the platform on Point Nepean Road.

KIDS AND FAMILIES

The pier is sturdy and features a railing down the length of the left hand side. The surrounding beach is also great for swimming.

FINALLY

A busy summer location with locals and visitors alike. The platform can produce some exceptional fishing when the water temperature rises and anglers implement the correct techniques.

ROSEBUD PIER

🔍 HOW TO GET THERE

Jetty Road, Rosebud. Travel along Point Nepean Road until you come to Jetty Road where a decent car park exists.

🔍 SNAPSHOT

PLATFORM
PIER

TARGET SPECIES
SQUID
GARFISH
FLATHEAD
SILVER TREVALLY

BEST BAITS
SILVERFISH, MAGGOTS, BLUEBAIT, SQUID, PILCHARD

BEST LURES
SOFT PLASTICS, SABIKI JIGS, SQUID JIGS

BEST TIMES
RISING TIDE IN LOW LIGHT CONDITIONS

SEASONS

Squid
Year round

Garfish
Winter and summer

Flathead
Summer

Silver trevally
Autumn

Rosebud Pier is a long structure built over predominantly shallow water. The pier isn't as productive as surrounding piers on the peninsula but when the squid and gars are around, bag limits can be achieved here.

TACTICS

Bring plenty of berley and a berley bucket if you plan on targeting garfish here. The lower landings at the end of the pier are most productive and bag limit captures are possible. Suspend baits under a pencil float and if you can see the fish but they aren't feeding – slowly reel your baits in as they will generally chase them down. Squid are best fished for after dark and it pays to fish under the lights for your best chance.

BAITS AND LURES

Silverfish and maggots both take their fare share of garfish but tiny slithers of pilchard also work well. Sabiki jigs are also popular with locals and when the garfish are thick, two or three can be caught at a time. The local squid population responds best to squid jigs in the 2.5 to 3.0 range and natural colours seem to work best.

BEST TIDE/TIMES

As the area is very shallow, it is best to fish here on a high tide. If you can only fish here during low tide, make sure you're fishing the final third of the pier. Calm winter evenings can produce some impressive bags of garfish.

AMENITIES

Public toilets, good car park and shops nearby.

KIDS AND FAMILIES

A good location to bring the kids as the pier is very sturdy and the beach is great for them to wade around in.

FINALLY

This can be a very handy option when the surrounding piers are busy with anglers and swimmers in summer.

McCRAE ROCK WALL (ANTHONY'S NOSE)

HOW TO GET THERE

Point Nepean Road, McCrae. Head south on Point Nepean Road until you see a wide gravel area that acts as the car park for cars with trailers for Anthony's Nose boat ramp. It is located at the base of Arthurs Seat.

SNAPSHOT

PLATFORM
BEACH/ROCK WALL

TARGET SPECIES
KING GEORGE
 WHITING
FLATHEAD
GARFISH
PINKIE SNAPPER
AUSTRALIAN SALMON
SQUID

BEST BAITS
SQUID, PIPI, MUSSEL, PRAWNS, BASS YABBIES, BEACH WORMS, BLUEBAIT, SILVER WHITING

BEST LURES
SOFT PLASTIC WORMS, SQUID JIGS

BEST TIMES
HIGH TIDE AT DUSK

The McCrae Rock wall, or Anthony's Nose as it is commonly known, is a hot spot for King George whiting during the summer months. The area is littered with weedbeds and sand patched that attracts a wide variety of morsels for the whiting to feed on. The area if relatively shallow thus it is best fished on a high tide, especially as the sun disappears.

TACTICS

The area is best fished with a light surf rod as it will allow you to reach some distances with your casts. If using braid, 8 to 10 lb line will be adequate, and should be attached to a 10 or 15 lb fluorocarbon leader. Depending on personal preference a running sinker or paternoster rig can be fished here. Best hooks include size 6 or 8 long shanks or circle hooks such as the Owner Mutu circle in size six. As there is no current in the area you should be able to get away with a 1 or 2 oz bomb sinker. Arrive before dark to see where the sand patches run through the interspersed weed and target your casts in these areas. If the area isn't full of anglers try casting a

silver whiting under a float for a shot at the squid in the area. Only position the bait 30 to 40 cm under the float though as it does get shallow and there is a chance of getting snagged on the bottom.

BAITS AND LURES

King George whiting do get pressured fairly heavily here in summer so it pays to have the freshest bait possible. Freshly caught squid or mussels purchased from the Safety Beach mussel farm do fare better than most other baits. In saying that though, pipi, Bass yabbies' and worms do well here too. For flathead try half or full bluebait over the sandy bottom. Garfish bite best on silver fish and can be targeted in the shallows here during the cooler months.

BEST TIDE/TIMES

The area is fairly shallow here thus a high tide is a must. As the water is generally clear in the area it is best to fish during low-light hours such as dawn, dusk and after dark. The whiting come into the shallows her under the guise of darkness so be prepared to fish throughout the night.

AMENITIES

There are no amenities in the immediate area.

KIDS AND FAMILIES

Not a bad place to take the kids; however they will need to be supervised at all times as the car park backs onto the main road.

FINALLY

A popular location with holiday goers during summer for King George whiting and for good reason too. Get there early to secure your spot.

SEASONS

King George whiting
November to March

Flathead
Summer

Garfish
Winter and spring

Pinkie snapper
Summer

Australian salmon
Summer

Squid
Summer

DROMANA PIER

🔍 HOW TO GET THERE

Point Nepean Road, Dromana. Take the Dromana exit from the freeway and turn left onto Point Nepean Road once you reach it. The pier is located approximately 900 m from here on your right hand side.

🔍 SNAPSHOT

PLATFORM
PIER

TARGET SPECIES
GARFISH
SQUID
KING GEORGE
WHITING
FLATHEAD
AUSTRALIAN SALMON

BEST BAITS
SILVERFISH,
MAGGOTS, SQUID,
PIPI, BLUEBAIT

BEST LURES
METAL LURES, SOFT
PLASTIC GRUBS AND
WORMS, SMALL
SQUID JIGS

BEST TIMES
HIGH TIDE

SEASONS
Garfish
Year round

King George whiting
Summer

Flathead
Warmer months

Squid
Year Round

Australian Salmon
Summer

Dromana Pier is surrounded by shallow water and a mainly sandy bottom. While you won't catch a 'big one' here you can experience some consistent catches of the fish that do inhabit the nearby waters.

TACTICS
Berley plays a vital role to success here so bring plenty of it. A berley cage can be dropped into the water via a rope attached to the pier which will help to attract fish such as garfish to the area. Use nibble tip rods with 4 lb mainlines which connect directly to a quill float and a size 12 long shank hook. Once the school of garfish is in the area you should be able to keep them around for a number of hours. King George whiting are not in abundance here due to a lack of structure for them to feed amongst but they swim up and down the entire length of the foreshore during summer. Cast a bait rod out with fresh squid or pipi for your best shot at tempting one. A running sinker rig will suffice as will a 10 lb leader and a small circle hook.

BAITS AND LURES
Silverfish and maggots are the best baits to use for garfish while King George whiting are best targeted with mussel and pipi in this area. Flathead are better targeted with a moving presentation that covers more ground so a soft plastic hopped along the sandy bottom is ideal. When the salmon are on metal lures are the go-to artificial offering here; however they can be targeted with a surf style paternoster rig when conditions are choppy.

BEST TIDE/TIMES
Due to the shallow nature of the beach here it's best to fish the pier during an incoming tide. Garfish can be found in big numbers during winter after dark for those brave enough to fish through icy conditions.

AMENITIES
The foreshore has recently been upgraded with a new playground and car park being established. BBQ facilities are also available as are take away shops across the road.

KIDS AND FAMILIES
Dromana Pier is a great place to take the kids to catch their first fish. They will need to be supervised on the pier at all times though as there is only a rail running along the left hand side. A playground is nearby if they get bored.

FINALLY
While not the most popular pier with anglers the platform does produce plenty of fish for those who fish it in the correct manner at the right times.

SAFETY BEACH BOAT RAMP JETTY

HOW TO GET THERE

If you're coming from the freeway take the Dromana exit and follow Nepean Highway until you hit the beach. Turn right at the intersection and follow Marine Drive for about a kilometre until you see the boat ramp and jetty on the left hand side.

SNAPSHOT

PLATFORM
JETTY

TARGET SPECIES
BREAM
PINKIE SNAPPER
GARFISH
FLATHEAD

BEST BAITS
SILVERFISH,
MUSSELS, BASS
YABBIES, MAGGOTS,
BEACH WORMS,
BLUEBAIT

BEST LURES
SOFT PLASTIC GRUBS
AND PADDLE TAILS

BEST TIMES
HIGH TIDE AT DAWN
OR DUSK

Boat ramp jetties are often overlooked as prime fishing locations however this one does receive a fair bit of attention during summer. While the area is devoid of any real structure, the pier pylons are covered with mussels which makes for a great feeding area.

TACTICS

Fish in this area are generally found hugging the jetty itself so it pays to keep casts short or along the pylons themselves. Garfish are best attracted with the use of a berley bucket filled with tuna oil soaked pellets. It can also pay to sporadically throw handfuls of berley out towards your baited floats. Bream tend to hand directly underneath the jetty and it can be a battle to try and coax one into eating a bait. Sending an unweighted mussel or Bass yabby down on a size 1 baitholder hook is your best option and remember to remain quiet once on the jetty. Pinkie snapper are occasionally mixed in with the bream and they too can be fished for in the same manner. Lock your drag up though – they'll head straight for the pylons if you do hook up.

BAITS AND LURES

For your best chance at tackling with one of the resident bream use light fluorocarbon leaders in the 4 to 6 lb range. It also pays to always have your rod in your hand rather than lying it on the pier as bites can be better detected. For a left field approach, try wading the surrounding shallows when safe to do so and cast small suspending hardbodies under the jetty. Garfish respond well to silverfish and maggots fished under a pencil float.

BEST TIDE/TIMES

As with most shallow water locations it pays to be fishing during low light conditions. Early mornings seem to be best for those chasing bream; however, garfish are best targeted at night. Incoming tides are generally best too.

AMENITIES

There are no amenities in the immediate area although shops and petrol stations are located nearby.

KIDS AND FAMILIES

A great jetty for kids to learn the craft of fishing. If things are slow the beach is excellent for swimming in so it's a win-win for all.

FINALLY

This little jetty offers some great bream fishing for those willing to put in the time and effort to catch them. The fish here are generally of good size which means they are quite old and it pays to employ catch and release methods for others to also enjoy.

SEASONS

Bream and Flathead
Summer

Pinkie snapper
Summer and autumn

Garfish
Winter and spring

MARTHA COVE BEACH

🔍 HOW TO GET THERE

Marine Drive, Martha Cove. Follow Marine Drive past Safety Beach and before reaching the Martha Cove underpass turn left into the Safety Beach Sailing Club car park.

🔍 SNAPSHOT

PLATFORM
BEACH

TARGET SPECIES
KING GEORGE WHITING
BREAM
PINKIE SNAPPER
FLATHEAD
SQUID

BEST BAITS
SQUID, PIPI, MUSSEL, BEACH WORMS, BLUEBAIT, PILCHARD, SILVER WHITING

BEST LURES
SQUID JIGS, SOFT PLASTICS

BEST TIMES
HIGH TIDE AFTER DARK

SEASONS

King George whiting
December to April

Bream
Summer

Pinkie snapper
Autumn

Flathead
Warmer months

Squid
Summer and autumn

This little beach has become quite popular since the rockwall that protects Martha Cove has been banned from fishing. While the beach is shallow it harbours some good weed patches that attract an array of species.

TACTICS

Light surf rods in the 10 ft range are most suited here to reach deeper water and the weed beds that intersperse throughout. There aren't many snags here so light lights and leaders are practical. To get the best distance use 8 or 10 lb braid on a 3000 or 4000 size reel along with a 1 or 2 oz bomb sinker at the base of your rig. Whiting are best targeted during dawn or dusk on a rising tide and a paternoster rig will suffice. Bream and pinkie snapper can also be fished for in the same manner. Squid are best targeted with a baited jig under a float after dark as they seek food and refuge amongst the weed. For the active angler; wade in up to your waist and cast plastics around for your chance to tangle with good sized flathead.

BAITS AND LURES

King George whiting are privy to fresh mussels here and it could be something to do with the mussel farm being in close proximity. In saying that though, pipi and squid will also produce fish. Bream are best targeted with beach worms here whilst flathead are best targeted with soft plastics bounced over the sand. Silver whiting threaded onto a squid prong seems to produce the best results on the local cephalopod population.

BEST TIDE/TIMES

Due to the shallow nature of the area the beach is best fished during low-light hours as the tide is coming in.

AMENITIES

A large car park facilitates the beach and public toilets are available at the yacht club. Bring your own food and drinks though as the closest shops are located in Dromana.

KIDS AND FAMILIES

The beach is very clean and the water is great for swimming in. Kids can muck about in the sand if they're not really into fishing.

FINALLY

A top location to fish when all of the piers are over flowing with anglers. The beach is extremely safe for children and can be extremely rewarding if the fish come to play.

MOUNT MARTHA CLIFFS

HOW TO GET THERE 🔍

Esplanade, Mount Martha. The cliffs run in front of Esplanade in Mount Martha and the best access points can be found at Ian Road, Bradford Road and Hearn Road.

SNAPSHOT 🔍

PLATFORM
ROCKS

TARGET SPECIES
SNAPPER
FLATHEAD
AUSTRALIAN SALMON
SQUID
GARFISH
KING GEORGE WHITING
LEATHERJACKET

BEST BAITS
SQUID, PIPI, MUSSEL, SILVER WHITING, PILCHARD, BLUEBAIT, SILVER FISH, MAGGOTS

BEST LURES
SQUID JIGS, SOFT PLASTICS, METAL SLUGS

BEST TIMES
TIDE CHANGE AT DAWN OR DUSK

This lengthy rock platform covers approximately three kilometres of coastline and produces a vast array of species year-round. While the track down to the cliffs is steep in some sections it is well worth the effort to get down.

TACTICS

For your best shot at tangling with a big snapper, head down during an onshore blow, particularly during dawn or dusk. It can get rough here during a strong westerly wind though so only head down if you feel comfortable doing so. A surf rod will aid in getting distance in your cast and it will also help you to lift fish up onto the rocks when it comes time to landing them. Most other species can be targeted with a paternoster rig and you don't have to cast far to get amongst them as the water drops to 3 or 4 m in front of the rocks. Casting squid jigs around weedy areas will be effective, as will sending out a silver whiting under a float. Garfish can be caught in big numbers by those who hang a berley bucket in the water to attract the schools. Fish with pencil float rigs and size 12 hooks to get amongst them.

BAITS AND LURES

Snapper are a big prospect here during rough weather and whole fish baits such as pilchard and silver whiting are good options for targeting them. Fresh fish fillets as well as squid can also be used to tempt them. The area is abundant with squid and they can be effectively fished for with squid jigs and baited jigs. Garfish are best fished for with silver fish or slithers of pilchard under a pencil float. You will need to berley to attract them to your area though. Australian salmon can be caught with soft plastics or metal slugs and can often be seen busting the surface.

BEST TIDE/TIMES

The best times to fish here will be dictated by the species you intend to target. Snapper and salmon are best fished for during or straight after a big onshore blow whereas calm weather is generally best for everything else. A changing tide will be most productive for all species.

AMENITIES

There are no amenities in the area apart from gravel car parks located sporadically along the cliffs.

KIDS AND FAMILIES

The cliffs are not suitable for young children as the rocks are only accessible via a steep hill. Teenagers will be able to navigate their way down.

FINALLY

One of the best landbased locations in Port Phillip Bay due to the wide variety of species on offer throughout the year.

SEASONS

Snapper
Spring and summer

Flathead
Summer

Australian salmon
Warmer months

Squid
Year round

Garfish
Year round

King George whiting
Summer

Leatherjacket
Year round

BALCOMBE CREEK BEACH

HOW TO GET THERE

Esplanade, Mount Martha. Park in one of the gravel car parks either side of Balcombe Creek.

SNAPSHOT

PLATFORM
BEACH

TARGET SPECIES
BREAM
MULLET
GARFISH
KING GEORGE
WHITING
PINKIE SNAPPER
AUSTRALIAN SALMON

BEST BAITS
PILCHARD, CHICKEN, SILVERFISH, SQUID, PIPI, MUSSEL

BEST LURES
METAL LURES, SOFT PLASTIC FLICK BAITS

BEST TIMES
RISING TIDE OR AFTER HEAVY RAINS WHEN THE MOUTH OF BALCOMBE ESTUARY IS OPEN

SEASONS

Bream
Summer

Mullet
Year round

Garfish
Year round

King George whiting
Dec. – April

Pinkie snapper
Autumn

Australian salmon
Summer

This picturesque beach is popular with swimmers and families during summer but anglers have not yet woken up to its fishing opportunities. When the creek mouth is open to the bay, a range of species will hang around in wait of any food mooching around the dirty water. The beach also experiences good runs of King George whiting and garfish during summer.

TACTICS

Light surf rods are ideal when chasing King George whiting and pinkie snapper. Two hook paternoster rigs will catch both species and long shank hooks are suitable for both species. Bring a couple of rod holders, sit the bait rods in them and wait for the rod tips to buckle over. Alternatively, flick soft plastics and metal lures around in search of local salmon schools. The fish won't be big but provide great sport for kids who are eager to get into the sport. When the mouth of the estuary is open keep an eye out for mullet foraging around in the shallows. Unweighted baits on light line will do the trick. Use a fine berley mix to attract local schools of garfish and set a size 12 hook just beneath a pencil float.

BAITS AND LURES

The local mullet population will readily take small pieces of dough or chicken while the garfish will happily take silverfish. King George whiting can be coaxed into taking squid strips, pipi and mussel and Australian salmon schools will readily chase down soft plastic flick baits and metal lures.

BEST TIDE/TIMES

A rising tide at dawn and into the night is best; however good fishing can be had throughout the day after heavy rains and wind has opened up the estuary mouth. For a relaxing evening, head down on a balmy night and bring the deck chairs.

AMENITIES

Public toilet block and shops are located nearby at Mount Martha shopping village.

KIDS AND FAMILIES

The beach area is a top place for kids and families to spend the day and local shops are just around the corner if they get bored.

FINALLY

A quiet beach location that can really turn on after heavy winds and rain have pounded the shore.

FISHERMAN'S BEACH BOAT RAMP

HOW TO GET THERE

Esplanade, Mornington. The fishing platform is located in the Fisherman's Beach boat Ramp car park on the Esplanade in Mornington. Look for the aptly named King George Avenue on the map.

SNAPSHOT

PLATFORM
RETAINING ROCK WALL/ROCKS

TARGET SPECIES
SQUID
PINKIE SNAPPER
AUSTRALIAN SNAPPER
ROCK COD
KING GEORGE WHITING

BEST BAITS
PILCHARD, BLUEBAIT, SAURIES, WHITEBAIT, SQUID, MUSSEL

BEST LURES
METAL LURES, SQUID JIGS

BEST TIMES
A HIGH TIDE ON DUSK

Fisherman's Beach Boat Ramp is a popular boat launching location in summer but a look to the bottom structure reveals a variety of rock and weed that fish use to feed and shelter in. Landbased anglers can take advantage of various species that call the area home in the warmer months by fishing the rocks at the point or from the retaining wall in the car park.

TACTICS

The areas located in front of the rocks the retaining rock wall is particularly reefy so be prepared to lose some tackle here. Heavier than normal leaders will need to be employed here and bomb sinkers are preferred over star varieties. Use a paternoster rig to keep baits off the bottom and try to arrive before the sun sets to get an idea of where sandy patches exist. The best method here is to bait and wait so either rest your rods against the retaining wall if fishing from the car park or wedge them between the rocks if fishing from the point. Surf rods are ideal for this location as long casts can be beneficial and the extra power will help to pull rigs out of snags. Squid can

be cast and retrieved to with artificial jigs but don't let them sink to bottom as they will get snagged. When the Australian salmon are in the area they can be caught by quickly retrieving metal slugs.

BAITS AND LURES

Snapper will happily take a well-presented pilchard, squid or silver whiting whereas King George whiting will take squid and mussel. Squid can be cast to with artificial squid jigs; however, silver whiting suspended under a float will also take a few. Australian salmon respond well to metal lures as well as bluebait and whitebait.

BEST TIDE/TIMES

A rising to full tide at dusk and into the night is best here. Arrive before the sun sets to get a better idea of what the underwater terrain is like.

AMENITIES

The car park is big enough to accommodate a number of cars and local shops are in close proximity. The beach is also nice and clean.

KIDS AND FAMILIES

Not the best location to take kids as the rocks can be slippery – Mornington Pier is a better option for keen young anglers. The beach is great for swimming in though.

FINALLY

Most anglers would forgo fishing here due to the popular Mornington Pier located nearby but some great species can be caught here during the warmer months.

SEASONS

Squid
Year round

Snapper
Spring and summer

Australian salmon
Winter

Rock cod
Cooler months

King George whiting
Summer

MORNINGTON PIER

HOW TO GET THERE

Schnapper Point Drive, Mornington. Head down Main Street in Mornington til you hit the roundabout at Esplanade. Head straight through and continue down Schnapper Point Drive until you reach the car park.

SNAPSHOT

PLATFORM
PIER

TARGET SPECIES
SQUID, KING GEORGE WHITING, GARFISH, SNAPPER, FLATHEAD, AUSTRALIAN SALMON

BEST BAITS
PILCHARD, BLUEBAIT, SQUID, PIPI, MUSSEL, SILVER FISH, MAGGOTS, SILVER WHITING, GARFISH

BEST LURES
SQUID JIGS, MINNOW STYLE SOFT PLASTICS

BEST TIMES
SUNRISE AND SUNSET DURING AN INCOMING TIDE

SEASONS

Squid
Summer and autumn

King George whiting
December to February

Garfish
Year round

Snapper
Spring

Flathead
Summer

Australian salmon
Autumn

Kingfish
Summer (sporadically)

The Mornington Pier provides anglers with access to deep water and reef in close proximity which ensures a vast array of species swim by. At the time of writing the Mornington Pier renovations have only been half completed. Despite the end of the pier being closed off for repair work this landbased location is still one of the best in Victoria.

TACTICS

To chase big snapper here you must be brave enough to fish during inclement weather; this means big onshore winds and waves that can potentially crash over the pier. Surf rods and reels that can hold 300 m of 20 lb line are best suited as big baits and sinkers need to be cast into head winds. Australian salmon can turn up to the pier in big numbers and anglers can have a ball chasing them on soft plastics and metal lures, particularly on the right hand side of the pier back towards the moored boats. Soft plastic rods in the 2 to 4 kg range with 6 lb line and 10 lb leaders will suffice for this style of fishing. Squid are often smaller here but when they're on – they're on and bag limit captures can be obtained in short time. If the big pier isn't producing try the smaller one in front of The Rocks restaurant.

BAITS AND LURES

For your best shot at snapper whole fish baits or fillets should be presented on either a paternoster or running sinker rig. Garfish are suckers for silver fish and maggots while squid strips and pipi are ideal for chasing King George whiting. When the Australian salmon are in close proximity to the pier they are best targeted with metal slugs or minnow style soft plastics. Kingfish do arrive here on occasions during summer and are best targeted with live baits such as garfish and squid but good luck stopping them if you do hook up.

BEST TIDE/TIMES

Big westerly winds that see the pier pounded by waves can produce some exceptional snapper fishing for those brave enough to venture out. Most other species fish best at dawn or dusk during an incoming tide. Calm weather and water is best suited to fishing for garfish and squid.

AMENITIES

Public toilets, a large car park and take away shops are all located at the start of the pier. Further up the hill before entering the car park is a playground and BBQ facilities for the family to enjoy.

KIDS AND FAMILIES

A great pier for kids providing they are supervised at all times. Families are often seen fishing here, especially during summer.

FINALLY

A top landbased location that is easily accessible to anglers. Once the repair work is complete the pier will once again be the best landbased location to target snapper on Port Phillip's eastern seaboard.

HOW TO GET THERE

Canadian Bay Road, Mount Eliza. Follow Canadian Bay Road through Mt Eliza village until you reach a cul de sac where parking is permitted.

SNAPSHOT

PLATFORM
ROCKS, BEACH

TARGET SPECIES
PINKIE SNAPPER
FLATHEAD
SQUID
KING GEORGE WHITING

BEST BAITS
PILCHARD, SQUID, SCAD, BLUEBAIT, PIPI

BEST LURES
SQUID JIGS, SOFT PLASTIC WORM PATTERNS

BEST TIMES
HIGH TIDE AT DUSK

Canadian Bay is one of those places that may take a while to work out but once you do, can be pretty special. The bottom structure is made up of rock and weed and a variety of species converge here during the warmer months.

TACTICS

It pays to bring a couple of different rods when fishing here: one lighter rod for soft plastic and squidding work, and a longer 10 ft rod for pitching baits with. Arrive before sunset and prospect along the rocks for squid. If you manage to catch a few make sure you keep one to use for fresh bait as the sun disappears. Don't let your jigs sink too long though as the area can be quite snaggy, particularly on a low tide. When fishing for whiting, pinkies and flathead use a paternoster rig tied from 10 to 15 lb leader. Calm conditions in summer will present the best opportunity for whiting, while a strong westerly wind puts you in with the best shot at catching pinkies. To best work out where to cast it pays to inspect the area when the sun is high.

BAITS AND LURES

Baits tend to work better than soft plastics here and it's worth bringing a few different kinds to see what the fish are best responding to. Scad fillets and chunk baits work extremely well here when the pinkies are around but they can make short work of bait, especially when the little guys are around. Other notable baits for pinkies are pilchard, squid and bluebait. Pipi and squid cocktail baits will tempt King George whiting and they can either be sent out on long shank hooks or circles depending on what you're more confident using.

BEST TIDE/TIMES

Calm conditions are ideal for King George whiting and squid whereas rough weather spurs the pinkie snapper on. Bigger high tides are also more favourable so fish around full and new moons when tide variations are greater. Dusk and into the night are the preferred times.

AMENITIES

There are no amenities in the immediate area; however, shops are located further up Canadian Bay Road so pick up supplies on your way down.

KIDS AND FAMILIES

The area isn't well suited to children as the rocks can be quite slippery at times. The beach isn't the best for swimming either as weed and rocks abounds the foreshore. The beach on the other side of the yacht club is much more suitable for swimming.

FINALLY

Spend the time to get to know the area and good bags of fish are definitely achievable. Fish in various conditions to gain an appreciation of what can be caught here.

SEASONS

Pinkie snapper
Summer and autumn

Flathead
Summer

Squid
Autumn

King George whiting
December to May

DAVEYS BAY

HOW TO GET THERE

Daveys Bay Road, Mount Eliza. Turn down Daveys Bay Road until you reach the small car park at the end. The beach is located a t the bottom of the stairs.

SNAPSHOT

PLATFORM
BEACH

TARGET SPECIES
KING GEORGE WHITING
PINKIE SNAPPER
FLATHEAD

BEST BAITS
SQUID, PIPI, BLUEBAIT, PILCHARD,MUSSELS

BEST LURES
SOFT PLASTICS

BEST TIMES
HIGH TIDE AT DUSK AND INTO THE NIGHT DURING A SOUTH WESTERLY WIND

SEASONS

King George whiting
Summer

Pinkie snapper
Summer and autumn

Flathead
Warmer months

This bay is popular with boaties when the King George whiting are in and they are often anchored less than 100 m from shore. Landbased anglers can get in amongst the action as the sun begins to drop and well into the night on a rising tide.

TACTICS

Long rods in the 9 to 11 ft range are ideal here as longer casts seem to attract more fish. Both paternoster and running sinker rigs will do the job here and leaders should be tied from 10 to 15 lb monofilament. Red tubing placed above the hooks work well as an extra attractant and lumo beads are effective after dark. If the pinkie snapper are in the area be prepared to lose plenty of bait to small fish but persis with them as there are usually some bigger models in the mix. Casting soft plastics over the shallow flats can produce good flathead at times.

BAITS AND LURES

Squid, pipi and mussel all work well on King George whiting and pinkie snapper will eat just about anything when they're feeding. Flathead respond well to soft plastics being hopped around in an erratic motion along the bottom.

BEST TIDE/TIMES

The best time to fish Daveys Bay and the majority of shallow beaches in Port Phillip Bay is around dawn and dusk or into the night. A rising tide also

AMENITIES

There are no amenities in the immediate area.

KIDS AND FAMILIES

A good location to take the kids and family as there is plenty of room for them to run around and the beach is quite good for swimming in.

FINALLY

A great King George whiting and pinkie snapper location during summer. Kick on after dark for best results.

OLIVERS HILL

HOW TO GET THERE

Nepean Highway, Frankston. Heading south on Nepean Highway, turn into the big car park that lies just before the incline of Olivers Hill begins. The main fishing platform can be accessed via a walking track from the car park that traverses the base of the hill.

SNAPSHOT

PLATFORM
ROCKWALL

TARGET SPECIES
KING GEORGE WHITING
SNAPPER/PINKIE
SNAPPER
GARFISH
FLATHEAD
SQUID

BEST BAITS
PILCHARD, PIPI, SQUID, BLUEBAIT, MUSSEL, SILVERFISH, SILVER WHITING

BEST LURES
ARTIFICAL SQUID JIGS

BEST TIMES
DAWN & DUSK DURING A RISING TIDE IS IDEAL FOR MOST SPECIES. BIG SPRING ONSHORE BLOWS ARE PRIME FOR BIGGER SNAPPER.

SEASONS

King George whiting
December to March

Snapper/Pinkie snapper
Spring and Autumn

Garfish
Winter

Flathead
Summer

Squid
Year round

Olivers Hill has always been well-recognised as a productive fishery for boaties but the landbased fishing can be red-hot too. The waters beneath the popular viewing point are littered with rock, reef and weed which support a wide variety of species.

TACTICS

It pays to have a couple of outfits in tow when fishing this location but time of year will generally dicate what is necessary. If snapper are on your wish list try fishing here during or directly after a big blow from the west. Surf rods are suited here as they aid in casting distance and they make it easier to land fish around the rocks. Main lines should consist of 20 lb braid or mono with leaders of 40 lb ideal. Sinker weight will vary with the conditions but generally speaking a 3 to 4 oz bomb or star is required to reach slightly deeper water. King George whiting can be targeted during the warmer months and it pays to get here during daylight to locate the sand holes between the reefy stuff. Aim your casts in amongst these holes for your best shot. Leaders can be tied from 10 lb and it always pays to add some red tubing or glow beads for after dark work. Squid can be caught while cast and retrieving squid jigs amongst the weed beds; however they can be fished for with a silver whiting suspended under a float. Garfish can be attracted in close with the use of berley and are best fished for with a pencil float rig. Flathead are usually a by-catch when fishing for whiting and snapper here.

BAITS AND LURES

If you're after bigger snapper use whole dead baits such as pilchards, bluebait, silver whiting and Californian squid. Pinkies will take the same just in half the portion sizes. King George whiting love fresh squid strips and pippies; however mussels also do the trick. Garfish only require small pieces of bait and silverfish make the perfect option. Squid jigs ranging from 2.5 to 3.5 are ideal on the local squid. Keep your ears out for reports of squid being caught in the area by the boaties.

BEST TIDE/TIMES

A rising tide around dawn or dusk is ideal here as the immediate area is rather shallow. Calm conditions are suited to fishing for whiting and squid whereas white caps and howling winds are perfect for any landbased snapper fisho. Bring the wet weather gear if you plan to fish in rough conditions as spray whips over the rocks here.

AMENITIES

A large car park services the area as does a public toilet. Shops are located five minutes up the road and bait can be purchased from the local servo if required.

KIDS AND FAMILIES

The area is ideal for keen young anglers although they must be supervised at all times as the rocks can get slippery. Frankston beach also provides a great area for swimming if you plan to fish here during the day.

FINALLY

A top location that can really turn it on at times. You just need to look at the area from the viewing point to realise its potential.

FRANKSTON PIER

HOW TO GET THERE

Nepean Highway, Frankston. Head south on Nepean Highway past Frankston shopping centre until you see a large carp ark located on the foreshore.

SNAPSHOT

PLATFORM
PIER

TARGET SPECIES
GARFISH
AUSTRALIAN SALMON
SNAPPER
FLATHEAD
SILVER TREVALLY

BEST BAITS
SILVER FISH,
MAGGOTS, PIPI,
SQUID, PILCHARD,
SILVER WHITING,
BLUEBAIT, WHITEBAIT

BEST LURES
METAL LURES,
BLADES, SOFT
PLASTICS

BEST TIMES
HIGH TIDE AT NIGHT

SEASONS

Garfish
Year round

Australian salmon
Autumn and winter

Snapper
Spring and summer

Flathead
Summer

Silver trevally
Autumn and winter

Frankston Pier is a long and stable platform that receives a wide variety of species throughout the year. Whilst it has always been a productive pier it has recently adopted an artificial reef located 40 m out from the end. This will no doubt increase its popularity, both with anglers and fish alike.

TACTICS

Australian salmon can be targeted during a big onshore blow with surf style rigs or metal lures. Focus on the channel that runs through the pier midway up its length. Big snapper can also be caught from the pier during or straight after a westerly blow in spring and summer. Targeting the new artificial reef which is located 40 m out from the end of the pier will be your best bet. Use surf rods to obtain longer casts and a long net or gaff to be able to land them. Best results will come after dark. Garfish can be targeted with a float rig along the entire length of the pier during calm conditions, especially at night. Target the shallows for flathead during summer by hopping soft plastics off the bottom.

BAITS AND LURES

When targeting salmon use metal lures in the 30 to 40 g range. Cast the lures as far as possible before retrieving them at a fast pace. They can also be targeted with bait on a paternoster rig with a surf popper on one dropper and half a bluebait on a 3/0 bait holder hook. Big snapper respond well to whole fish baits such as pilchard, silver whiting and garfish. Use bait elastic around pilchards to help them stay on longer. Soft plastics are best for flathead, especially in the shallows during summer

when the water temperatures are peaking. Silver fish and maggots suspended under a float are best for garfish.

BEST TIDE/TIMES

High tide is best for most species here. For snapper and salmon fish during a strong westerly wind and around a new moon if they coincide during spring.

AMENITIES

Frankston foreshore features a playground, large car park and public toilets. A restaurant is also situated at the start of the pier.

KIDS AND FAMILIES

A great pier for the kids and family especially with the foreshore being in tip-top condition. The pier provides a great platform for the kids to catch their first fish.

FINALLY

A great landbased location to chase a wide range of species from and with the introduction of the artificial reef it is sure to be one of the best in years to come.

SEAFORD PIER

HOW TO GET THERE

Nepean Highway, Seaford. Seaford pier is located directly opposite the shops on Nepean Highway in Seaford. Park in the car park opposite Station Street.

SNAPSHOT

PLATFORM
PIER

TARGET SPECIES
GARFISH
FLATHEAD
FLOUNDER
MULLET

BEST BAITS
SILVER FISH,
MAGGOTS, PIPI,
PRAWN

BEST LURES
SOFT PLASTIC SHADS
AND PADDLE TAILS,
SABIKI RIG

BEST TIMES
DAWN OR DUSK

S eaford Pier is a bit of a hidden gem; popular with locals for targeting garfish. The pier runs out over a mainly sandy bottom that drops into about two metres towards the end.

TACTICS

The most effective way to target garfish is with berley and a float rig. Tie the rig from 6 lb leader, a quill float and a size 12 long shank hook. You will need to add some split shot sinkers near the hook to ensure the float sits upright in the water column. Establish a good berley trail of fine bran or Weet-Bix mixed with tuna oil and once you attract them to your area you should be able to keep them around for hours. Flathead are best targeted with soft plastics around the sand bars that run near the pier. Target the drop offs on either side of the sand bars and fish during an incoming or outgoing tide. Flounder are best targeted on the surrounding beach after dark during a low tide with a spot light and hand spear. *Please note: The use or possession of a hand-held spear is prohibited within 30 m of any jetty.*

BAITS AND LURES

Garfish only have small mouths so silver fish and maggots are perfect when suspended under a float. If you cannot get your hands on either try small pieces of prawn, pipi or pilchard. Flathead are best targeted with soft plastics either from the pier or if wading close to the pier. They tend to hang on the drop offs formed by the sand bars so primarily target these areas. Flounder are also prominent around these sand bars and require the use of a spot light and spear after dark in calm conditions.

BEST TIDE/TIMES

Garfish can be caught throughout the entire tide cycle so long as berley is employed. For best results though fish during low-light hours such as dawn or dusk. An incoming or outgoing tide is best for flathead and will dictate which side of the sand bar they sit. During an incoming tide fish the side closest to the shore while an outgoing tide will see them sitting on the farthest side to the shoreline.

AMENITIES

The area has recently been upgraded and features public toilets, a car park and a café. A supermarket and more take away stores are located directly across the road.

KIDS AND FAMILIES

Seaford beach is one of the cleanest on the eastern seaboard and is a great place to take the kids for a swim. The pier is also very stable and safe so long as the little ones are supervised at all times.

FINALLY

While there isn't a huge array of species to target here Seaford Pier does produce a lot of garfish for bait or the table.

SEASONS

Garfish
Year round

Flathead
Summer

Flounder
Summer

Mullet
Year round

PATTERSON RIVER

🔍 HOW TO GET THERE

The main river arm can be reached via Launching Way which is located off McLeod Road. The river mouth is facilitated by a car park just off Stephens Road.

🔍 SNAPSHOT

PLATFORM
VARIOUS

TARGET SPECIES
BREAM
YELLOW-EYE MULLET
GARFISH
MULLOWAY
AUSTRALIAN SALMON
PINKIE SNAPPER

BEST BAITS
PRAWNS, SCRUB WORMS, PILCHARD, BASS YABBIES, FRESHWATER YABBIES, BREAD, LIVE MULLET, GARDEN WORMS

BEST LURES
SOFT PLASTICS, METAL LURES, VIBES, SHALLOW RUNNING HARDBODIES

BEST TIMES
TIDE CHANGES ARE MOST PRODUCTIVE

SEASONS

Bream
Year round

Yellow-eye mullet
Year round

Garfish
Summer

Mulloway
Summer and autumn

Australian salmon
Winter and spring

Pinkie snapper
Summer and autumn

Patterson River is a popular fishery that facilitates one of, if not the most popular boat ramp in Victoria. The river system feeds the private lake systems and holds good numbers of fish on a year-round basis.

TACTICS

Your target species will dictate where you fish in the river system so it pays to have a target in mind. Focus around the mouth of the river if you're after a mixed bag as Australian salmon, bream, mullet, garfish and the occasional pinkie snapper can be caught from here. Work your way from the rail bridge down to the entrance for best results on these various species. Further up the system, around the boat ramps and gates is best for targeting bream, mulloway and mullet. A pencil float rig with a size12 hook is best when targeting mullet and garfish whereas a running sinker rig is ideal for bream and pinkie snapper. Metal lures work best around the mouth of the river for salmon but they will also take whitebait on a paternoster rig. Mulloway should be targeted around tide changes, preferably at night.

BAITS AND LURES

Bream will take a variety of baits in the river but they are quite fussy so fresh is best. Prawns, Bass yabbies and small freshwater yabbies are all good baits. Salmon will take whole whitebait and pieces of bluebait on a paternoster rig but metal slices and soft plastic stick baits are better suited. Mullet and garfish respond well to plenty of berley so use a fine mix of pellets and tuna oil to attract them to your area. Fish bread dough, silverfish and maggots for best results. Mulloway are tough customers to crack but for your best chance use live mullet or shallow running hardbodies.

BEST TIDE/TIMES

The river system is highly affected by tides so with that in mind it pays to be fishing around tide changes at both the low and high phases. Fishing early in the morning and late in the afternoon produce good results especially around the new moon.

AMENITIES

BBQ facilities, walking tracks and a small tackle store facilitate this great fishery. Shops aren't too far away either so food and drink can be obtained quite easily.

KIDS AND FAMILIES

This would have to be one of the best locations along the bay to take kids and families. There is plenty of space for the kids to run around in and walking tracks abound the river for those who don't mind a bit of exercise.

FINALLY

Patterson River is a popular waterway and makes for the perfect place to spend the day.

HOW TO GET THERE 🔍

Nepean Highway, Chelsea. Park your car in any of the beach car parks along Nepean Highway.

SNAPSHOT 🔍

PLATFORM
BEACH

TARGET SPECIES
FLATHEAD

BEST BAITS
BLUEBAIT, SQUID

BEST LURES
SOFT PLASTIC CURL TAIL GRUBS, SHALLOW DIVING HARDBODIES, BLADES, LIPLESS CRANKBAITS

BEST TIMES
LOW LIGHT PERIODS DURING SUMMER

While many wouldn't associate a beach such as this with fishing, some big flathead can be caught around the gutters that run parallel to the shore. By actively covering as much ground as possible, anglers can come across some 50 cm plus fish. The best part is – the kids can run around the beach or go for a swim while you catch dinner.

TACTICS
Wading the shallows makes for a good option in order to reach the deeper gutters that run parallel to the shore. Soft plastics and blades are proven flathead catchers and they should be worked on 1/8 oz jigheads close to the bottom. Cast the lures as far as possible – with a particular focus around drop offs – before slowly hopping the plastics up and off the bottom. Don't go too fast as flathead will try to exert as little energy as possible when obtaining a feed. The aim is to make your lure look injured as the fish see it as an easy meal. Bait fishing can also produce a few fish but it pays to keep casting in different areas until you find a fish or two. It definitely pays to be active when fishing extensive beaches such as this one.

BAITS AND LURES
Flathead love a moving target so soft plastics, blades and shallow diving hardbodies are ideal. Lipless crankbaits also work a treat on the ambush predators. For those that prefer to use bait, try bluebait and squid on 2/0 baitholder hooks.

BEST TIDE/TIMES
Tide changes make for optimum times to fish for flathead that lie in gutters as they sit in wait to ambush food that travels over the sand bar. Summer sees good concentrations of fish in the area so to avoid the swimmers fish at dawn or late dusk.

AMENITIES
There are plenty of shops and cafes along Nepean Highway along the main strip of Chelsea.

KIDS AND FAMILIES
Kids love the beach and this one is great for swimming in so bring them along and if they aren't keen anglers, they can spend the day in the shallows.

FINALLY
This type of fishing won't be for everyone but the biggest Port Phillip Bay flathead are often caught in a metre or less of water – give it a go and you may just surprise yourself.

SEASONS
Flathead
Warmer months

MORDIALLOC PIER

🔍 HOW TO GET THERE

Beach Road,
Mordialloc.

🔍 SNAPSHOT

PLATFORM
PIER

TARGET SPECIES
SNAPPER
AUSTRALIAN SALMON
GARFISH
MULLET
BREAM
KING GEORGE
WHITING
SILVER TREVALLY
SQUID

BEST BAITS
SILVER WHITING,
WHOLE SQUID,
CUTTLEFISH, SLIMY
MACKEREL, PIPI,
BLUEBAIT, PILCHARD,
SILVER FISH,
MAGGOTS

BEST LURES
SQUID JIGS, SOFT
PLASTICS, VIBES,
METAL LURES

BEST TIMES
STRONG SOUTH
WESTERLY WINDS
DURING LOW-LIGHT
HOURS

SEASONS

Snapper
Spring and summer

Australian salmon
Summer

Garfish
Winter and spring

Mullet
Year round

Bream
Year round

King George whiting
Summer and autumn

Silver trevally
Winter

Squid
Summer and autumn

In recent years Mordialloc Pier has become the number one landbased structure to target big snapper from. This may be the case due to several outstanding snapper seasons or because a knowledgeable band of anglers know when best to chase them. Either way, it's impressive!

TACTICS

The best spot to fish for snapper is at the very end of the pier but good luck getting a spot. The local experts get their places early and you'll be waiting a while for them to leave. Use surf rods to target the reef that runs along the right hand side of the pier and put in the time during big onshore blows in spring. Both running sinker and paternoster rigs will work. Tie them from 30 or 40 lb leader matched with 5/0 suicide hooks. You won't always be rewarded but when you do you'll know about it. Bring a long gaff or drop net to land the fish. Use plenty of berley to attract gars and mullet to your area and a pencil float rig with a size 12 hook will be adequate. Target the reef on the right hand side of the pier for both King George whiting and squid.

BAITS AND LURES

Big snapper like fresh baits so if you can catch your own bait do so. Garfish, mackerel, squid and cuttlefish all account for some big snapper here but if you can't catch your own bait try whole pilchards, silver whiting and Californian squid. Garfish can be caught on silver fish and maggots while mullet respond well to dough and small pieces of chicken.

Australian salmon will take metal slugs with gusto but will also hit whitebait and bluebait. Use artificial jigs amongst the reef for squid.

BEST TIDE/TIMES

A big south westerly wind during spring is the prime time for snapper especially after dark. Most other species are best targeted during a tide change.

AMENITIES

The pier has plenty going for it including a large car park with a kiosk that is open during the warmer months. A park is located nearby which houses public toilets and a playground. The shopping strip along Main Street is only a five minute walk away too.

KIDS AND FAMILIES

Mordialloc Pier is a great place to take the kids and family. The beach is great for swimming in and a nearby park features a playground that they can lose themselves in. Public toilets are also close by.

FINALLY

A consistent landbased location that can produce some exceptional catches if the right techniques are employed.

PARKDALE BEACH

FACT BOX – HOW TO GET THERE Follow Beach Road on from Mordialloc Pier and park between Rennison Street and McIndoe Parade.

SNAPSHOT

PLATFORM
BEACH

TARGET SPECIES
PINKIE SNAPPER
KING GEORGE WHITING
FLATHEAD
AUSTRALIAN SALMON

BEST BAITS
SQUID, PIPI, PILCHARD, BLUEBAIT, SAURIES

BEST LURES
SOFT PLASTIC GRUBS AND CREATURES

BEST TIMES
HIGH TIDE AFTER DARK

While it may not look like much to the naked eye, this stretch of beach can be extremely productive during the warmer months. A vast array of weed beds are interspersed amongst sandy stretches which makes for perfect hunting grounds.

TACTICS

When fishing beaches such as this one it pays to arrive during daylight to gain an understanding of where the bottom structure lives. Bring a couple of rods with you – one for bait and one for working lures with. Something in the 9 to 11 ft range will suffice for bait fishing as you'll need to obtain some distance with your casts. Match the rod up with a 3000 to 4000 size reel and load it with 10 lb braid. Aim to land your casts in the sandy patches between the weed and focus most of your fishing attention around a high tide. With a shorter graphite rod it pays to flick soft plastics around in search of pinkie snapper and flathead. Flathead love a moving lure so keep your retrieves constant but subtle. Australian salmon will often roam the area during winter and will happily take soft plastics and metal lures.

BAITS AND LURES

King George whiting love cocktail baits so it pays to lace either a size 6 long shank or small circle hook with a pipi and squid strip. Use a paternoster rig tied from 15 lb fluorocarbon and finished off with a 1 oz bomb sinker. This rig will put you in the running for pinkie snapper and flathead too but a running

sinker rig is also ideal. Soft plastic grubs are also great for prospecting these types of beaches with and they should be mounted on a 1/4 oz jighead to aid with casting distance. Allow the lure to sink to the bottom before slowly retrieving with gentle hops in between.

BEST TIDE/TIMES

The area is shallow and features a number of sand bars that run parallel to the shore so high tide is best. A high tide that coincides with dawn/dusk or into the night is ideal, so too is fishing three days either side of a new or full moon.

AMENITIES

There are no amenities in the immediate area.

KIDS AND FAMILIES

The stretch of beach is barren but it's a good place to take the kids for a swim during the day. With that in mind though, the best fishing occurs during low-light hours. Mordialloc Pier is a better location to take the kids.

FINALLY

These beaches are very underrated and many anglers drive past them without a second look. Spend some time here during warm summer evenings for best results.

SEASONS

Pinkie snapper
Spring to autumn

King George whiting
Summer

Flathead
Summer

Australian salmon
Winter

BEAUMARIS YACHT SQUADRON JETTY

🔍 HOW TO GET THERE

Beach Road, Beaumaris. Park in one of the side streets along beach road (Ray Street or Cromer Road) and cross Beach Road before entering the Yacht Squadron area through the gate. You cannot park down the ramp here unless you are a member of the Motor Yacht Squadron.

🔍 SNAPSHOT

PLATFORM
PIER

TARGET SPECIES
SQUID
SNAPPER
PINKIE SNAPPER
GARFISH
KING GEORGE
WHITING
AUSTRALIAN
SALMON

BEST BAITS
SQUID, MUSSEL, PIPI, SILVER WHITING, PILCHARD, SAURIES, SILVER FISH, MAGGOTS

BEST LURES
SQUID JIGS, METAL SLUGS, SOFT PLASTICS

BEST TIMES
HIGH TIDE AT SUNRISE OR SUNSET.

SEASONS

Squid
Spring

Snapper
Spring

Pinkie snapper
Summer and autumn

Garfish
Year round

King George whiting
Warmer months

Australian salmon
Winter

TACTICS

The area immediately surrounding the pier is made up of reef and weed and as such provides great habitat for squid. Slow sinking squid jigs are a good idea here, so too is counting down the sink rate beside the pier to work out how long to let the jig sink before retrieving. An egi rod is ideal as the extra casting distance will allow your jig to cover more ground. Snapper fishing is best from the end of the pier casting directly out during a big southwesterly in spring and summer. Surf rods will aid in casting distance and landing fish. Tie your rig from 30 or 40 lb leader with two snelled 5/0 hooks. Garfish are best targeted during calm conditions and a float rig is ideal. Look for sand patches amongst the reef when targeting King George whiting here.

BAITS AND LURES

Best snapper baits include whole Californian squid, squid strips, silver whiting, garfish and pilchard. King George whiting will eat pipi and squid cocktail baits while garfish respond best to silverfish and maggots. Berley is a must if you want to keep them in the area. When Australian salmon schools are in the area it's time to bring out the metal lures and high speed spinning will do the job. Soft plastic stickbaits can also be cast and retrieved towards the school.

BEST TIDE/TIMES

Strong westerly winds promote snapper to feed in the shallows here and some exceptional catches can be taken here for those brave enough to venture out. Squid and garfish are best targeted on an incoming tide when conditions are calm.

AMENITIES

There are no amenities in the immediate area.

KIDS AND FAMILIES

A good place to take the kids provided they are supervised at all times as there is only a rail along one side.

FINALLY

While only small in stature, this pier has plenty to offer with a variety of species to target.

HALF MOON BAY JETTY

HOW TO GET THERE

Beach Road, Black Rock. Travel along Beach Road until you see the sign for Half Moon Bay boat ramp.

SNAPSHOT

PLATFORM
PIER

TARGET SPECIES
KING GEORGE
WHITING
SNAPPER
PINKIE SNAPPER
SQUID

BEST BAITS
SILVER WHITING,
PILCHARD, BLUEBAIT,
SLIMY MACKEREL,
MUSSEL, SQUID, PIPI,
SAURIES

BEST LURES
SQUID JIGS

BEST TIMES
HIGH TIDE AFTER
DARK

While the platform is only small at Half Moon Bay, the rewards can be big for those who put the time and effort in. Every year some big snapper get caught from here thanks to the deeper water and reef that surrounds the H.M.V.S Cerberus.

TACTICS

Surf rods and reels capable of holding 200 m of 20 lb line are highly recommended here as you will need to punch your baits out towards the H.M.V.S Cerberus during onshore winds. The Cerberus provides a great place for snapper to feed in the shallows hence the reason for casting baits in the area. Single dropper paternoster rigs tied from 40 lb leader with snelled 5/0 hooks should be more than enough to stop snapper here. Circle hooks will allow the fish to hook themselves and anglers can just look out for rod buckles rather than taps on the rod tip. This is handy as deciphering small bites from wave action during strong winds can be difficult. King George whiting can be caught around the weed beds here and squid and pipi should be used on a paternoster rig tied from 15 lb leader.

BAITS AND LURES

Snapper like fish baits such as silver whiting, pilchard and sauries. Wrap your baits with bait mate or use salted varieties to help the baits stay on the hooks for longer. King George whiting prefer soft mushy baits such as pipi, mussel or tenderized squid strips.

BEST TIDE/TIMES

The best time to fish is during a big south westerly blow at the start of spring. While conditions are uncomfortable they do provide the prime time to fish for big red. King George whiting and squid are best targeted on warm calm nights in summer.

AMENITIES

A fish and chip shop and restaurant is located on the foreshore here and is a popular eatery during summer. Car parks can be a rarity in the warmer months during the day so be early to avoid disappointment.

KIDS AND FAMILIES

Not the best place to take the kids as the pier is small and there isn't much else to do.

FINALLY

The jetty here provides a great location for landbased snapper in the right conditions. Get here early when a south westerly is blowing during spring for the best spot at the end of the pier.

SEASONS

King George whiting
Summer and autumn

Snapper
Spring

Pinkie snapper
Summer

Squid
Summer

HALF MOON BAY ROCKS

HOW TO GET THERE

Beach Road, Black Rock. Park in the car park at the bottom of the hill and head in the opposite direction of the pier towards the beach where you will see a set of rocks.

SNAPSHOT

PLATFORM
ROCKS

TARGET SPECIES
SNAPPER
FLATHEAD
GARFISH
AUSTRALIAN
SALMON
KING GEORGE
WHITING

BEST BAITS
BLUEBAIT, SQUID,
PIPI

BEST LURES
METAL LURES, SOFT
PLASTIC GRUBS

BEST TIMES
HIGH TIDE AT DUSK.

SEASONS

Snapper
Spring and summer

Flathead
Summer

Garfish
Winter and summer

Australian salmon
Winter

King George whiting
Summer

While the pier attracts its fair share of anglers, the rocks in front of the car park and along the beach are more productive for a wide range of species. Spend some time exploring the rocky areas and listen out for reports of snapper in the area – they can be caught from here early in spring when conditions are wild.

TACTICS

If you want to tangle with a decent snapper you'll have to brave the elements in early spring and fish the area during or just after a strong westerly wind. Paternoster and running sinker rigs work equally as well as eachother bit the bottom structure is quite snaggy so be prepared and pre-tie some rigs before you leave home. Hooks should be in the 4/0 to 5/0 range and whole baits are ideal. Garfish can be attracted to the area with handfuls of berley thrown in at regular intervals and they are best fished for with a pencil float rig. King George whiting frequent the area over the summer period and can be caught with size 6 long shank hooks laced with squid or pipi. Cast baits into the sand holes between the reef for your best shot.

BAITS AND LURES

Flathead will take just about anything but bluebait and squid seem to be the best options when it comes to bait. Soft plastics tend to work better on flatties so try something like a curl tail grub or paddle tail slowly worked along the bottom structure. Garfish can be caught with silverfish suspended under a pencil float and King George whiting are best fished for with pipi or squid. Snapper can't resist pilchards

and silver whiting but whole Californian squid works just as well.

BEST TIDE/TIMES

The area isn't very deep so a high tide during low light periods is best as fish feel more comfortable feeding when they have a bit of cover over their heads. Garfish can be caught throughout the day here but for your best shot at King George whiting and snapper, kick on after dark.

AMENITIES

There is a good car park and fish and chip shop. Bring change here though as there are parking meters and restrictions until 8pm.

KIDS AND FAMILIES

The pier is more comfortable for children but they should be able to navigate the rocks in front of the car park and along the beach without too much fuss.

FINALLY

The rocks are more productive than the pier here but there are plenty of snags around so be prepared to lose some tackle. Give the area a shot in spring during a strong southwesterly as plenty of snapper get caught here each year.

SANDRINGHAM BREAKWALL

HOW TO GET THERE

Jetty Road, Sandringham. Follow Beach Road until you come across Jetty Road in Sandringham. The breakwall is located behind the footy oval.

SNAPSHOT

PLATFORM
ROCKWALL

TARGET SPECIES
FLATHEAD
SNAPPER
GARFISH
KING GEORGE
WHITING

BEST BAITS
PILCHARD, BLUEBAIT, SQUID, CUTTLEFISH, TUNA FILLET, SILVER WHITING, RED ROCKETS, SILVERFISH

BEST LURES
SOFT PLASTIC GRUBS, PADDLE TAILS AND CREATURES

BEST TIMES
TIDE CHANGE AT SUNSET

The Sandringham Breakwall is often forgotten about by many anglers when snapper season arrives as Brighton Breakwall and Mordialloc Pier seem to steal the limelight. This shouldn't be the case as the area around the rockwall is littered with reef and deeper water which makes for perfect early season snapper grounds.

TACTICS

If snapper are your target then it's time to bring the surf rods out. They will not only help to punch out long casts but they will also make it easier to control the fish with once you get them close to the wall. A long gaff or landing net is also required to land them. Use 20 to 40 lb mainline and heavier leaders in the 50 to 60 lb range are ideal to contend with snags and abrasion from rocks. Snelling two hooks to the end of your leader is best however a single 5/0 hook will also suffice. Find a place between two rocks to stand your rod in but make sure it's secure as a big fish could easily take your rod in on its first run. For King George whiting and flathead you'll only require a 7 ft rod in the 3 to 5 kg range. If fishing the inside of the breakwall only use a small amount of lead as the water is generally calm in here. Throw soft plastics around the boats and pylons for your best shot at flathead and bream.

BAITS AND LURES

Big snapper love big baits so it pays to send out whole fish such as pilchard, silver whiting, red rockets and bluebait. They are also privy to fresh squid or cuttlefish if you can get your hands on some. Go for a hardier bait where you can as you'll be casting into strong winds and snaggy terrain most of the time. King George whiting will eat mussels, pipi and squid strips while flathead will eat a range of soft plastics. Garfish can be attracted

with berley and they are best fished for with silverfish under a pencil float rig. Bream in this area are suckers for soft plastic crabs fished alongside the pylons and underneath the moored boats.

BEST TIDE/TIMES

For your best shot at tangling with a big snapper it pays to fish during or straight after a big westerly blow. Casting into a strong head wind can be quite difficult but thankfully the fish come in close to feed around the rocky structure. If King George whiting or flathead are your preferred targets then calmer conditions are better and they can often be targeted on the inside of the breakwall where the boats are moored.

AMENITIES

There are no amenities in the area so it pays to be prepared before arriving.

KIDS AND FAMILIES

Not the best location for kids due to the rocky nature of the fishing platform. They can be hard to navigate at the best of times so care must be taken if you decide to bring little ones here.

FINALLY

The breakwall is an underrated location that can provide some big fish when the conditions are right. Put in the hours during uncomfortable conditions and you may just surprise yourself.

SEASONS

Flathead
Summer

Snapper
Spring & summer

Garfish
Winter & summer

King George whiting
Summer

Bream
Year round

HAMPTON ROCK GROYNES

🔍 HOW TO GET THERE

Beach Road, Hampton. The rock platforms are located at the end of Ne Street and Orlando Street.

🔍 SNAPSHOT

PLATFORM
ROCKS

TARGET SPECIES
SNAPPER
FLATHEAD
GARFISH
SQUID

BEST BAITS
SILVER WHITING, PILCHARD, GARFISH, SQUID, SILVERFISH

BEST LURES
SOFT PLASTIC GRUBS, VIBES, SQUID JIGS

BEST TIMES
IF YOU'RE AFTER BIG SNAPPER TRY FISHING DURING OR STRAIGHT AFTER A SOUTHWESTERLY BLOW BUT ONLY WHEN IT IS SAFE TO DO SO

SEASONS

Snapper
Spring and summer

Flathead
Summer

Garfish
Year round

Squid
Autumn

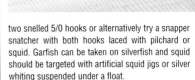

Two rock walls jut out from the beach along beach road in Hampton and they both provide great fishing opportunities in the right conditions. The rocks are easily accessible and reasonably simple to fish from. Big snapper are the major draw card here during spring.

TACTICS

Surf rods in the 10 to 12 ft range are ideal here as long casts are imperative when chasing snapper. The longer rods will also help to pull fish up over the rocks when landing bigger specimens. When chasing snapper it pays to have a 4000 to 6000 size reel loaded with 20 lb mainline and a leader of 40 to 50 pound. Star sinkers in the 3 to 5 oz range may be necessary to hold bottom when conditions are rough and 5/0 hooks are preferred. Keep in mind that you will need to either hold your rod or wedge it between rocks when fishing here. If you intend to fish after dark make sure you have good lighting, as the rocks can be tricky to navigate once the sun drops. Casting squid jigs in calm weather can be productive as can soft plastics for the local flathead. Garfish can be berleyed up right next to the rocks and a float setup is ideal.

BAITS AND LURES

Typical snapper baits of silver whiting and pilchard are best here. Use full fish baits and rig them on two snelled 5/0 hooks or alternatively try a snapper snatcher with both hooks laced with pilchard or squid. Garfish can be taken on silverfish and squid should be targeted with artificial squid jigs or silver whiting suspended under a float.

BEST TIDE/TIMES

A rising to full tide is best here. For your best chance at snapper fish during or just after a strong southwesterly blow.

AMENITIES

There are no amenities in the immediate area.

KIDS AND FAMILIES

May be suitable for teenagers but not small kids due to the rocky platform that can get slippery after heavy rains.

FINALLY

A top landbased location for big reds – especially at the start of spring when the fish are feeding in the shallows. Keep an eye out for reports of snapper in the Sandringham and Brighton area.

BRIGHTON BEACH

HOW TO GET THERE 🔍

Esplanade, Brighton. Park along the Esplanade between the Brighton Savoy and Dendy Street.

SNAPSHOT 🔍

PLATFORM
BEACH

TARGET SPECIES
PINKIE SNAPPER
KING GEORGE WHITING
LEATHERJACKET
FLATHEAD

BEST BAITS
BLUEBAIT, PIPI, SQUID, MUSSEL, PILCHARD

BEST LURES
SOFT PLASTIC CURL TAIL GRUBS

BEST TIMES
RISING TIDE AT DAWN OR DUSK

SEASONS
All species
Summer

This section of beach is often overlooked as a fishing location due to its popularity with swimmers and kite surfers. A quick glance at Google Maps indicates that a rocky/weedy terrain lives underneath the surface. This provides suitable habitat for a number of species and the best part about it all – it's all within casting distance of the shore.

TACTICS

The shallow water immediately in front of the foreshore is littered with scattered rock and weed which makes for great shorebased fishing. Light surf outfits are well suited here and something in the 10 to 12 ft range is ideal. Sinker weights will vary depending on conditions but you should be able to get away with a 1 or 2 oz bomb sinker on most occasions. A two hook paternoster rig will be effective on all species and should be tied from 12 to 15 lb leader. Aim your casts in the sandy patches between the rock and weed for your best shot at tangling with the shallow goodies. Soft plastics can also be presented amongst the sandy stretches, particularly at dawn and dusk. By doing so you'll put yourself in with a shot at the local flathead and pinkie snapper populations.

BAITS AND LURES

Pinkie snapper and flathead are suckers for bluebait, squid and soft plastics. Present bluebait in half on a size 1 baitholder hook or 2/0 circle hook depending on what you're more confident with. Curl tail grubs in the 3 to 5 inch range rigged on a 1/4 oz jighead also make for good options. Retrieve with short sharp hops along the bottom. King George whiting are privy to fresh squid, pipi and mussel as are leatherjacket.

BEST TIDE/TIMES

A rising tide at dawn or dusk is best but fishing into the night can also be productive. Target the times around the new and full moon for best results. King George whiting will generally bite in 15 to 30 minute patches so when they're on it pays to hold your rod at all times.

AMENITIES

There are no amenities along the beach; however, it is only a short walk to the Brighton Sea Baths which contains a café and toilets.

KIDS AND FAMILIES

The beach is popular with swimmers and beach goers so the kids can have a muck around in the shallows if they're not that into fishing.

FINALLY

A top location that produces a tasty variety of fish during the summer months. Dedicate the time to work out patterns and really achieve some great results.

BRIGHTON BACKWATER

🔍 HOW TO GET THERE

Esplanade, Brighton. Follow the Esplanade in Brighton and turn into the car park opposite Normanby Street.

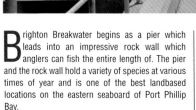

🔍 SNAPSHOT

PLATFORM
PIER/ROCK WALL

TARGET SPECIES
FLATHEAD
SNAPPER
PINKIE SNAPPER
KING GEORGE
 WHITING
SQUID
GARFISH
GUMMY SHARKS

BEST BAITS
SALTED PILCHARDS, BLUEBAIT, SILVER WHITING, SQUID, PIPI, SILVER FISH, MAGGOT

BEST LURES
SOFT PLASTICS, BLADES, SQUID JIGS

BEST TIMES
EVENING ON A HIGH TIDE

SEASONS
Flathead
Year round
Snapper
Spring
Pinkie snapper
Summer and autumn
King George whiting
December to April
Squid
Autumn
Garfish
Year round
Gummy sharks
Year round

Brighton Breakwater begins as a pier which leads into an impressive rock wall which anglers can fish the entire length of. The pier and the rock wall hold a variety of species at various times of year and is one of the best landbased locations on the eastern seaboard of Port Phillip Bay.

TACTICS
Depending on the species you are after will very much dictate when to fish here and what gear you should bring. If specifically targeting big snapper fish during a big westerly blow throughout spring in low-light hours for your best shot. Surf rods with 20 to 30 lb main lines attached to a 40 lb paternoster rig will suffice. Fish from the last hut on the pier to the end of the rock wall and bring a long net or gaff to land them. There are plenty of snags on the area so you will need to keep them high up in the water column once hooked. Squid are best targeted near the sea baths located to the left of the pier and King George whiting can be found in the same area. Cast soft plastics and vibes on the inside of the rock wall towards the moored boats for your best shot at flathead.

BAITS AND LURES
Whole fish baits are best when targeting snapper, especially salted pilchards or bluebait. Wrap your baits with bait mate to ensure they stay on during long casts. Artificial squid jigs in size 2.5 and 3 are best here – use bright jigs during the day and dark jigs at night for best results. Fresh squid and pipi will tempt the local King George whiting here while soft plastics and vibes are best for the flathead.

BEST TIDE/TIMES
Big westerly blows, high tides and diminishing light provide the perfect combination for snapper in spring. Evening high tides are ideal for squid and whiting whereas flathead and garfish will bite throughout the day.

AMENITIES
A car park is located directly in front of the pier although parking fees do apply. A café is also located on the foreshore here.

KIDS AND FAMILIES
There is a lot of room for the kids at this location; however, they will need to be supervised at all times, especially if you plan to take them on the rock wall.

FINALLY
A very productive location that can offer some big fish at certain times of year. Be persistent and prepared to sit through some inclement weather and the rewards will come.

HOW TO GET THERE

Jacka Boulevard, St Kilda. The pier is located at the end of Fitzroy Street in the heart of St Kilda's cultured centre.

SNAPSHOT

PLATFORM
PIER AND ROCKS

TARGET SPECIES
SNAPPER
FLATHEAD
GARFISH
GUMMY SHARKS

BEST BAITS
PILCHARD, BLUEBAIT, SQUID, SILVERFISH, MAGGOTS, SALMON FILLETS, TUNA

BEST LURES
SOFT PLASTICS

BEST TIMES
A HIGH TIDE EARLY IN THE DAY OR INTO THE NIGHT

S t Kilda Pier and Breakwater is popular amongst city fishers and a range of species can be caught from here. The platform becomes extremely busy during summer, especially with tourists so night time can be the best time to fish here.

TACTICS

When targeting snapper, surf rods are recommended as they will help to cast baits into deeper water. The extra length will also help to navigate fish around pylons when it comes to the landing stage. Make sure you bring a long net or gaff as the pier sits quite high off the water level. Lighter surf rods and paternoster rigs are ideal when chasing flathead and pinkie snapper and a 15 lb leader will suffice. Use a two hook rig and mix the baits up to see what the fish are best responding to. If gummy sharks are your target species, fish into the night and use surf rods with reels capable of holding 200 to 250 m of 20 lb mainline. Rigs should consist of 40 lb leader and hooks in the 4/0 to 6/0 range. Patience will play a big role in achieving success here.

BAITS AND LURES

Snapper can be caught with larger baits such as silver whiting, pilchard, bluebait and whole Californian squid. Garfish will take silverfish and maggots suspended under a pencil float and flathead will redily take bluebait and squid. Soft plastics hopped along the bottom will catch their fare share of flathead and pinkie snapper. If you want to have a go at a landbased gummy shark, use fishy baits like salmon and tuna and persist long into the night.

BEST TIDE/TIMES

A rising tide is most productive here, especially around dusk and into the night. Garfish, flathead and pinkie snapper can be caught throughout the day here but a tide change is a must.

AMENITIES

The area is well serviced with cafés, restaurants, shops and toilets.

KIDS AND FAMILIES

A great location to spend the day as shops and cafes are located nearby. The pier is wide and extremely stable so kids have some space to muck around too.

FINALLY

A productive location that is easily accessible for city dwellers. Parking can be expensive for the day here so be prepared.

SEASONS

Snapper
Spring and summer

Flathead
Warmer months

Garfish
Year round

**Gummy sharks
Summer**

KERFERD ROAD PIER

🔍 HOW TO GET THERE

Beaconsfield Parade, Albert Park. Follow Beaconsfield Parade towards Port Melbourne until you hit Kerferd Road.

🔍 SNAPSHOT

PLATFORM
PIER

TARGET SPECIES
SNAPPER
FLATHEAD
KING GEORGE
WHITING
GUMMY SHARK
GARFISH

BEST BAITS
PILCHARD, BLUEBAIT, SQUID STRIPS, PIPI, MUSSEL, SILVER FISH, MAGGOTS, SILVER WHITING, TUNA FILLET, SALMON CUTLETS

BEST LURES
SOFT PLASTICS, VIBES

BEST TIMES
INCOMING TIDE

SEASONS

King George whiting
Warmer months

Gummy shark
Summer

Garfish
Year round

Snapper
Summer and autumn

Flathead
Year round

Kerferd Road Pier is a consistent fishery for those that know how to fish it. Locals line the pier on any given day and walking the length of the pier gives you the feeling that there's something special about this place.

TACTICS

Surf rods are ideal for targeting snapper and gummy sharks with as they provide some grunt and the extra length makes it easier to manage the fish around the pier. Something in the 10 to 12 ft range with a rating of 10 kg or thereabouts is ideal. Match the rod with a 4000 to 6000 size reel and load it up with 20 lb main line and a 40 or 60 lb leader. Single dropper paternoster rigs will suffice and 5/0 and 6/0 hooks are ideal. Patience is imperative when targeting these species from the shore so be prepared to fish throughout the night. A new moon is ideal for snapper whereas a full moon is more suited to targeting gummy sharks. The bottom is mainly sandy here so there isn't a lot of structure to target when it comes to chasing whiting. Mid-way along the left hand side of the pier seems to produce the best numbers of these fish though.

BAITS AND LURES

Big baits catch big fish so it it's snapper or gummy sharks that you're after; use bigger baits. Snapper will take whole squid, pilchards, silver whiting and bluebait while gummy sharks prefer oilier baits such as tuna and salmon. King George whiting will eat pipi, squid and mussel; however, bluebait slithers is also a good option for them here. Garfish are best fished for with small offerings such as silver fish and maggots and plenty of berley is required to keep them in your area. Flathead can be caught on half baits of pilchard and bluebait but hopping soft plastic grubs or vibes along the bottom is your best bet.

BEST TIDE/TIMES

As is the case with most landbased fisheries, the bigger fish come out to play after dark during a high tide. A tide change during the day will produce a fair share of fish too.

AMENITIES

The pier is situated in a fairly popular area thus shops and cafés are in close proximity. Public toilets can also be found along Beaconsfield Parade.

KIDS AND FAMILIES

The pier is stable and features a rail along most of its length. The beach is good for swimming too if the kids get bored.

FINALLY

A great place to unwind for a leisurely fish or for the more serious anglers, there is a real possibility of hooking into a big red here.

LAGOON PIER

HOW TO GET THERE 🔍

Beach Street, Port Melbourne. Head north west along Beaconsfield Parade until it turns into Beach Street. Lagoon Pier is situated directly opposite Esplanade East.

SNAPSHOT 🔍

PLATFORM
PIER

TARGET SPECIES
SNAPPER
GUMMY SHARKS
FLATHEAD
GARFISH

BEST BAITS
SILVER WHITING, TUNA, SALMON, CURED EEL, SILVERFISH, BLUEBAIT, PILCHARD, GARFISH, SILVER TREVALLY

BEST LURES
SOFT PLASTIC GRUBS AND WORMS

BEST TIMES
DURING OR DIRECTLY AFTER A BIG SOUTHWESTERLY WIND – ESPECIALLY ON A HIGH TIDE AFTER DARK

SEASONS

Snapper
Spring and summer

Gummy sharks
Summer

Flathead
Warmer months

Garfish
Year round

Lagoon Pier and Kerferd Road Pier fish very similarly but if you were to choose between the two for a chance at big fish, Lagoon would be the winner. Plenty of big snapper are caught from this structure around Christmas and for this reason it has gained in popularity over the past few years.

TACTICS

Light graphite rods are well suited to casting soft plastics around for flathead and something in the 7 ft range will be ideal here. Load the rod with a 2500 reel and some 8 lb braid and you're good to go. Jighead weights will be dictated by conditions but you won't have to go any heavier than 1/8 ounces. Long surf rods are practical for snapper as they can send baits out a long distance and they will help when it comes to landing big fish. Gummy sharks should be fished for with the same tackle and are often a by-catch for anglers when fishing for snapper. Leader material should be in the 40 lb range and 5/0 to 6/0 hooks are ideal. Concentrate your efforts from the bend in the pier to the end.

BAITS AND LURES

Silver whiting, garfish, red rockets, sauries, squid and tuna are all good baits for snapper while salmon, cured eel and trevally are best suited to gummy sharks. Garfish can't resist silverfish and flathead will take just about anything but bluebait and soft plastics are best.

BEST TIDE/TIMES

Fish into the night for snapper and gummy sharks. Tide changes will prove most effective and strong southwesterly winds will bring the fish into the shallows. Garfish can be caught throughout most of the tide and flathead will be most active on the run out tide.

AMENITIES

There are public toilets located on the foreshore with cafes, kiosks and restaurants all nearby.

KIDS AND FAMILIES

A sturdy platform for kids to fish from but it is quite narrow so they will have to be supervised at all times. The beach is good for swimming in during summer and there are plenty of nearby shops and cafes.

FINALLY

One of the best landbased locations to chase big snapper from but get here early to claim your position.

SANDRIDGE BEACH ROCK GROYNES

HOW TO GET THERE

The Boulevard, Port Melbourne. The rock groynes can be found along The Boulevard between Todd and Beacon Roads.

SNAPSHOT

PLATFORM
ROCKS

TARGET SPECIES
SNAPPER
FLATHEAD
LING
MULLOWAY
BREAM

BEST BAITS
BASS YABBIES, PRAWNS, BLUEBAIT, PILCHARD, SAURIES, SQUID

BEST LURES
BLADES, VIBES, SOFT PLASTICS, BIG SHALLOW RUNNING HARDBODIES

BEST TIMES
A HIGH TIDE AT DUSK IS PRIME TIME FOR THE MAJORITY OF SPECIES

SEASONS

Snapper
Spring

Flathead
Summer

Ling
Year round

Mulloway
Year round

Bream
Year round

The rock groynes extend out from the beach here and both provide anglers with a great opportunity to tangle with some great species. The bottom structure is most sand but some big snapper and mulloway cruise through the area when conditions are right. Patience and determination will go a long way to achieving success here.

TACTICS

Surf rods are ideal here as they will allow you to cast baits out into deeper water and if you manage to hook up to a snapper or resident mulloway, you'll need the extra power. Snapper and mulloway are best fished for after dark and fresh baits are the key. Running sinker rigs are ideal for both species and leaders should be between 20 and 40 pound. Neither species is particularly easy to catch from the shore so be prepared to put in plenty of hours. Casting barramundi style lures after dark can also coax mulloway into an aggression type bite so give it a go. Ling are a regular by-catch in the area and while they don't look all that attractive; they taste great. Bream should be targeted with soft plastics and blades hopped around structure but lightly weighted Bass yabbies will take their fare share of fish.

BAITS AND LURES

Fresh baits are best for snapper and if you can catch some fresh squid or mullet you'll be in with a good chance at catching an elusive Melbourne mulloway.

Bass yabbies are the best bait for bream although peeled prawns also work well. Flathead will eat a wide range of soft plastics cast but bluebait will also do the trick.

BEST TIDE/TIMES

Like most landbased locations around Port Phillip Bay, low light conditions combined with a rising tide is best. Try your luck after dark for your best chance at tangling with something big, red or silver.

AMENITIES

There is good parking, a playground and BBQ facilities located along the shore.

KIDS AND FAMILIES

The rocks are relatively easy to navigate as they are fairly flat but kids will constantly require supervision. The park located along The Boulevard will keep them entertained if they get bored.

FINALLY

If you're a local, take the time to really work the place out as patterns will emerge. If you're visiting for the first time, focus your efforts around a full moon after dark but bring suitable lighting.

HOW TO GET THERE 🔍

The Strand, Newport. The Warmies is located south west of the West Gate Bridge and parking can be found along The Strand. The area gets particularly busy with boat traffic during snapper season.

SNAPSHOT 🔍

PLATFORM
ROCKS/JETTY

TARGET SPECIES
BREAM
MULLOWAY
TAILOR
SNAPPER
MULLET
FLATHEAD
AUSTRALIAN SALMON

BEST BAITS
BASS YABBIES, LIVE MULLET, PEELED PRAWNS, PILCHARD

BEST LURES
LARGE SHALLOW RUNNING HARDBODIES, BLADES, SOFT PLASTICS

BEST TIMES
ON AN INCOMING TIDE OR WHEN THE POWER STATION IS PUMPING HOT WATER INTO THE SYSTEM.

SEASONS

Bream
Year round

Mulloway
Year round

Tailor
Winter and spring

Snapper
Spring and summer

Mullet
Year round

Flathead
Summer

Salmon
Winter and spring

The Warmies is one of the most popular landbased locations around Port Phillip Bay mainly due to the species on offer and its capability to accommodate plenty of anglers. When the local power station is running, hot water is pumped into the system, which attracts large numbers of bait, and the predatory species are usually close behind. A wide variety of methods can be implemented here, making it ideal for anglers of all skill levels.

TACTICS

The Warmies suits two types of angler in particular – those who like to sit back, relax and soak a bait and those who prefer to walk around while flicking lures. Soft plastic rods in the 3 to 5 kg range will suit most applications for lure anglers and a mixture of blades and soft plastics can be thrown. Jighead weights should range from 1/32 to 1/8 oz and it pays to mix up plastic profiles as different species prefer different styles. The area is fairly devoid of any prominent structure so focus your attention around tide changes when species such as bream will be most active. Bait anglers can set up a number of rods with running sinker and paternoster rigs both as productive as each other. Float rigs are also ideal for the local mullet population. Berley will promote fish to feed in your area so give yourself an advantage and throw handfuls of pellets in at constant intervals. Mulloway are viable targets here and live mullet either suspended under a float or allowed to swim unweighted will put you in with a good chance. When the tailor and Australian salmon are around it is time to cast and retrieve small metal lures around.

BAITS AND LURES

Bass yabbies and peeled prawn will do well on bream while mullet will take dough fished under a float rig. Snapper can be fished for with pilchard as can flathead but live mullet can also be effective – as many anglers have found out when fishing for mulloway. Casting a variety of soft plastics and vibes is effective on most species here so actively flick lures around rather than standing in the one spot.

BEST TIDE/TIMES

The best time to be fishing here is hen the power outlet is pumping hot water out but a tide change is ideal at all other times. Fish into the night for your best chance at a Melbourne mulloway.

AMENITIES

The area is serviced by a large car park, public toilets, big park areas and BBQ facilities.

KIDS AND FAMILIES

The area is great for kids as they can spend the day at the park if the fishing is slow. Keep an eye on them when fishing the rocks as they can be unstable or slippery after rain.

FINALLY

The Warmies has earned a great reputation for producing fish but it can be overfished at times so try to stay away from the crowds.

FERGUSON STREET PIER

🔍 HOW TO GET THERE

Pier Street, Altona. The pier is located down the end of the bustling Pier Street. Parking can be found close by along the Esplanade.

🔍 SNAPSHOT

PLATFORM
PIER

TARGET SPECIES
SNAPPER
SQUID
FLATHEAD
KING GEORGE
WHITING

BEST BAITS
SILVER WHITING,
PILCHARD, GARFISH,
SAURIE, TUNA, SQUID,
PIPI

BEST LURES
SOFT PLASTICS,
SQUID JIGS

BEST TIMES
A RISING TIDE
DURING LOW LIGHT
HOURS. FISH LATE
INTO THE NIGHT
DURING HEAVY
WINDS FOR YOUR
BEST CHANCE AT A
SNAPPER.

SEASONS

Snapper
Spring and summer

Squid
Autumn

Flathead
**Year round but
summer is best**

King George whiting
Summer

Ferguson Street Pier plays host to plenty of moored boats which provide shelter and food for the local fish population. Bream are the main draw card here but locals can often be found chasing mullet and garfish. The pier boasts great views of the city and makes for a relaxing environment to cast a line.

TACTICS

Float fishing is very productive here as garfish and mullet can be found in great numbers here. Rigs should be made up of a pencil float, a size 12 hook and some split shot sinkers crimped along the line. Spinning outfits can be used for this method of fishing but long telescopic poles are purpose built for float fishing. Bream should be targeted around the pylons and unweighted Bass yabbies, mussel and prawns make for gun baits. Vertically vibing around the pier's structure also produces great umbers of fish but lock your drag up as bream will dust you around the pylons in an instant. Snapper can be fished for by casting baits out into the deeper water and running sinker rigs are ideal. Surf rods might be useful for snapper as you'll need some pulling power around the base of the pier. Mulloway have been known to swim by the area so try your luck around a full moon with a live mullet hanging off the end of your line. Heavy gear will be required to stop them though as they will head straight for structure once they realized they are hooked.

BAITS AND LURES

Bream will take Bass yabbies', mussel and peeled prawns while snapper will eat pilchard, silver

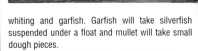

whiting and garfish. Garfish will take silverfish suspended under a float and mullet will take small dough pieces.

BEST TIDE/TIMES

Tide changes present the best opportunity to tangle with the local bream population. All other species can be caught throughout the day and night but calm weather and clear water make for the best conditions.

AMENITIES

Plenty of parking is available close by and public toilets can be accessed along The Strand. Cafes can be found up the road too should you need a coffee or some food to get through a long fishing session.

KIDS AND FAMILIES

A great place to take the kids, especially when the garfish and mullet are in big numbers.

FINALLY

A productive pier situated amongst picturesque surroundings.

WILLIAMSTOWN BEACH ROCKWALL

HOW TO GET THERE

Esplanade, Williamstown. The rockwall is located at the end of Victoria Street and is serviced by a large car park.

SNAPSHOT

PLATFORM
ROCKS

TARGET SPECIES
SQUID
SNAPPER
AUSTRALIAN SALMON
KING GEORGE WHITING
LEATHERJACKET
FLATHEAD

BEST BAITS
SQUID, PIPI, WHITEBAIT, BLUEBAIT, PILCHARD, SILVR WHITING

BEST LURES
SQUID JIGS, METAL LURES, SOFT PLASTICS

BEST TIMES
HIGH TIDE AT DAWN OR DUSK.

The rockwall can facilitate a large number of anglers and does get busy during the warmer months when a range of tasty species inhabit the local waters. The bottom is made up of rocky reef and weed beds which attracts some of Port Phillip bay's best eating fish.

TACTICS

Target the sand patches between the rock and weed for your best chance at King George whiting. A 7 ft rod should do the trick but a 9 to 11 ft rod can help to achieve longer distances. Surf rods are ideal for pitching bigger baits out for bigger species such as snapper – try after dark on a rising tide for best results. Squid can be fished for with silver whiting under a float or with squid jigs cast and retrieved from the rocks. Concentrate your efforts over the weed beds and bring a net to help you land them. Leatherjacket are a tasty species worth fishing for here and they can be caught with long shank hooks laced with pipi pieces on a paternoster rig. Aim your baits around the rocky structure but strike quick as they have a habit of stealing bait.

BAITS AND LURES

King George whiting bite best on cocktail baits of pipi and squid strips while leatherjacket will take the same baits but in smaller portions. Australian salmon can turn up from time to time and metal lures will do the trick if you can see them feeding on the surface. Snapper should be fished for with bluebait, squid and pilchard and silver whiting suspended under a float will take squid around the weed beds.

BEST TIDE/TIMES

A rising tide around dawn and dusk and into the night will be most productive. Bring the head lamps with you after dark as you'll need the light to navigate around the rocks.

AMENITIES

There are public toilets, a good car park and shops nearby.

KIDS AND FAMILIES

The rocks can be slippery so supervision is a must. A wide variety of species can be caught here though so they should stay entertained.

FINALLY

A productive location that puts anglers within easy access of a variety of species. Bring a variety of outfits along, as you never know what might turn up on any given day.

SEASONS

Squid
Year round

Snapper
Spring

Australian salmon
Winter

King George whiting
Summer

Leatherjacket
Year round

Flathead
Warmer months

ALTONA PIER

🔍 HOW TO GET THERE

Pier Street, Altona.
The pier is located
down the end of the
bustling Pier Street.
Parking can be found
close by along the
Esplanade.

🔍 SNAPSHOT

PLATFORM
PIER

TARGET SPECIES
SNAPPER
SQUID
FLATHEAD
KING GEORGE
WHITING

BEST BAITS
SILVER WHITING,
PILCHARD, GARFISH,
SAURIE, TUNA,
SQUID, PIPI

BEST LURES
SOFT PLASTICS,
SQUID JIGS

BEST TIMES
A RISING TIDE
DURING LOW LIGHT
HOURS. FISH LATE
INTO THE NIGHT
DURING HEAVY
WINDS FOR YOUR
BEST CHANCE AT A
SNAPPER.

SEASONS

Snapper
Spring and summer

Squid
Autumn

Flathead
**Year round but
summer is best**

King George whiting
Summer

Altona Pier has become one of Port Phillip Bay's standout locations for landbased snapper. The pier is popular during the summer months and provides plenty of room for a large number of anglers. Arrive early to get the best spot at the end of the pier.

TACTICS

Snapper fishing from piers generally requires the use of a surf rod to not only obtain long casts into deeper water, but to be able to control fish around pier pylons. A long net or gaff is required here as you won't be able to dead lift a big fish up onto the platform. Fishing for snapper is most successful after dark and running sinker rigs tied from 40 lb leader are ideal. Don't be too quick to strike when you notice a bite as the snapper can be finicky early on in the season. Circle hooks can be beneficial as can reels with a baitrunner mode. Flathead can be targeted along the vast sand flats towards the start of the pier and flicking soft plastics around should pluck a fish or two. King George whiting can be caught around the weed beds and a paternoster rig tied from 10 lb will suffice. Flicking squid jigs around the same weedy areas will produce a few squid from time to time. Look for any ink on the pier to reveal their location.

BAITS AND LURES

Fresh baits are best for snapper and silver whiting, tuna strips, pilchard, garfish and squid will all do the trick. King George whiting can be taken on squid, pipi and mussel while flathead are best fished for with soft plastics – curl tail grubs and paddletails are best.

BEST TIDE/TIMES

The area is fairly shallow until the last section of the pier so a rising to high tide is best, particularly at dusk and into the night. Fish around the new moon during snapper season for your best shot at Port Phillip Bay's iconic 'big red'.

AMENITIES

There are toilets, shops, cafes and a great beach all in close proximity.

KIDS AND FAMILIES

Kids will love the expansive sandy area along the beach here and the fishing platform is safe too. If they get bored, there are plenty of shops and things to do on Pier Street.

FINALLY

The pier can accommodate plenty of anglers along its length which certainly adds to its appeal. Listen out for reports of fish being taken around Millers Reef and put the hours in after dark.

WERRIBEE RIVER

HOW TO GET THERE

Beach Road, Werribee South. The main section of the river can be found along Beach Road in Werribee where a boat ramp and jetty services the area. Further up the river, anglers can find access from K-Road.

SNAPSHOT

PLATFORM
PIER/BEACH

TARGET SPECIES
BREAM
MULLET
MULLOWAY
TREVALLY
AUSTRALIAN
SALMON

BEST BAITS
BASS YABBIES, SANDWORMS, CHICKEN, DOUGH, LIVE MULLET, PEELED PRAWN, PIPI

BEST LURES
SOFT PLASTICS, BLADES, METAL LURES, SMALL HARDBODY LURES

BEST TIMES
HIGH TIDE IN THE MORNING OR DURING OVERCAST DAYS.

SEASONS
All species
Year round

Werribee River is a popular landbased location and anglers can fish from a range of structures. The river has established itself as one of Melbourne's most consistent bream fisheries.

TACTICS

Soft plastic style rods are perfect for this location and they should be matched with 2500 size reels with 4 to 8 lb braid. Bream are quite clever so light presentations are best, especially when bait fishing. Runnng sinker rigs are great for bream and they should be tied from 6 lb fluorocarbon leaders. Use as little weight as possible and strike at the slightest of twitches in your line as bream can be stealthy biters. If lures are more your thing, cast around likely looking areas with soft plastics, blades and hardbodies. Work your way up and down the bank and pitch lures towards any structure you can find. Popular areas to focus your attention include the K-Road cliffs and around the moored boats near the mouth of the estuary. Mullet can be fished for with a light float rig and hooks should be quite small

– a size 10 or 12 long shank should be sufficient. Mulloway are a viable target here and they can be fished for with blades, soft plastics and live mullet. Stay on after dark for your best chance at tangling with Melbourne's finest.

BAITS AND LURES

Bream will take live Bass yabbies as well as sandworms with gusto. If you can't get your hands on any, try peeled prawns or pipi. Mullet can be fished for with dough or small pieces of chicken under a float and if you manage to catch a few send one out live for a mulloway.

BEST TIDE/TIMES

Early mornings combined with a rising tide seem to be best for most species here. Bream are most active during a tide change so plan your trip around the tides.

AMENITIES

Public toilets, playground and BBQ facilities.

KIDS AND FAMILIES

With such a wide area to fish and plenty of room to run around, Werribee River makes for a fantastic place to bring the kids for the day.

FINALLY

A great place to spend the day at with plenty of fish on offer and the chance at an elusive Melbourne mulloway.

GRAMMAR SCHOOL LAGOON

🔍 HOW TO GET THERE

Foreshore Road, Corio, Geelong. Fish east of the boat ramp – the channel can be recognised quite easily thanks to buoys and markers.

🔍 SNAPSHOT

PLATFORM
BEACH

TARGET SPECIES
SNAPPER
BREAM
FLATHEAD
SHARKS
AUSTRALIAN
SALMON

BEST BAITS
SILVER WHITING,
GARFISH, TUNA,
PILCHARD, FRESH
SQUID

BEST LURES
SOFT PLASTIC
GRUBS, CREATURES
AND WORMS, METAL
LURES

BEST TIMES
RISING TIDE INTO
THE NIGHT.

SEASONS

Snapper
**Winter through to
summer**

Bream
Year round

Flathead
Warmer months

Sharks
Year round

Australian salmon
Winter

A channel running parallel to the shore sees big fish cruising through and in casting distance of landbased anglers. Big snapper are the main draw card here especially during the winter months.

TACTICS
The best option here is to simply bait and wait. Use surf rods to reach the shipping channel from the shore and then sit back and wait for the rod tip to buckle over. 2 to 3 oz bomb sinkers will hold bottom here and 4/0 to 6/0 hooks on 40 lb leader will do the job nicely. If you're after bream, try flicking soft plastics and blades around or if bait is more your thing, use a light running sinker rig over the weed and sand flats. Australian salmon can occasionally cruise through here during winter so it pays to have some metal lures in the tackle bag.

BAITS AND LURES
Snapper can't resist fresh bait and if you can manage to catch some squid you could be in for a treat here. Silver whiting, garfish, pilchard and tuna fillets will also do the job so don't be afraid to experiment. Bream will take soft plastic creatures, worms and grubs and Australian salmon are easy to fool with metal lures.

BEST TIDE/TIMES
High tides are best as the channel fills up with more water that fish feel safe to navigate in. Try after dark during winter for your best chance at tangling with a genuine five kilo plus snapper. Gummy sharks can also be encountered here throughout the year so hang on if you manage to hook one.

AMENITIES
There are no amenities in the immediate area so bring plenty of food and water if you plan to stay a while.

KIDS AND FAMILIES
A safe location to bring the kids but can become boring if the fish aren't biting as there isn't much here for them to do.

FINALLY
A top location to fish with the possibility of tangling with big fish on offer. Bring the deck chairs and rod holders and wait for the drags to start screaming.

NORTH SHORE ROCKS

HOW TO GET THERE

The Esplanade, North Shore, Geelong. The area is fairly non-descript but the rocks are located at the base of The Esplanade and parking is available on the side of the road here.

SNAPSHOT

PLATFORM

PLATFORM
ROCKS

TARGET SPECIES
FLATHEAD
AUSTRALIAN
SALMON
SNAPPER

BEST BAITS
SILVER WHITING,
PILCHARD, BLUEBAIT,
SQUID, WHITEBAIT

BEST LURES
SOFT PLASTIC
STICKBAITS, METAL
LURES

BEST TIMES
LOW TIDE AROUND
DAWN AND DUSK
AND INTO THE NIGHT

While this area may not look too appealing; there can be some great fishing on offer during summer. It is a great location to fish when low tide coincides with dawn or dusk.

TACTICS

Surf rods are ideal here as you'll need to get the bait away from the rocks and reef that sits tight to the fishing area. Main lines of 15 to 20 lb will suffice as will 30 to 40 lb leaders. A paternoster rig is usually best when trying to achieve distance and a 2 to 3 oz bomb sinker will be enough to hold bottom here. Australian salmon can turn up in big numbers here at times and metal lures cast and retrieved at a quick pace will see them undone.

BAITS AND LURES

Silver whiting, pilchard, bluebait and whole squid will attract snapper while flathead cant resist smaller pieces of the same bait. Australian salmon will chase down metal lures with gusto but they can also be targeted with whitebait and bluebait.

BEST TIDE/TIMES

Unlike most landbased locations, this one is best fished at low tide as high tide can actually cover the fishing platform. Low light periods are best but some decent snapper do get caught here during the day too.

AMENITIES

There are no amenities available in the immediate area so take in what you need.

KIDS AND FAMILIES

Not a good location for kids as the walk down in steep and the rocks can be very slippery at times.

FINALLY

A location worth persisting with as some good fishing can be had. Fishing at low tide is a must.

SEASONS

Flathead
Warmer months

Australian salmon
Winter and spring

Snapper
Spring and summer

MOORPANYAL PARK BEACH

🔍 HOW TO GET THERE

The Esplanade, North Shore, Geelong. Travel along The Esplanade in North Shore until you see the sign for Moorpanyal Park.

🔍 SNAPSHOT

PLATFORM
BEACH AND ROCKS

TARGET SPECIES
KING GEORGE WHITING
SNAPPER
FLATHEAD

BEST BAITS
SQUID, PIPI, PEELED PRAWN, BASS YABBIES, BLUEBAIT

BEST LURES
SOFT PLASTIC GRUBS

BEST TIMES
HIGH TIDE AROUND DUSK AND INTO THE NIGHT.

SEASONS

King George whiting
Summer

Snapper
Spring and summer

Flathead
Warmer months

This picturesque beach isn't regularly spoken about in landbased fishing circles but it does offer some top fishing for those that put in the time here. The location is made up of a weedy bottom and fishing can take place from the sand or rocks scattered throughout the area.

TACTICS

Lighter surf rods are perfect here and casting into the sandy patches between the weed is a must. King George whiting frequent the area due to its broken reef terrain and they are best fished for with a paternoster rig tied from 10 to 15 lb leader. Pinkie snapper can be fished for in the same manner but rather than using long shank hooks, try baitholders or circle hooks in the 2/0 size range. Flathead can also be caught on the same tackle but soft plastics hopped along the sandy flats makes for a better option.

BAITS AND LURES

King George whiting can be fussy at times so it pays to have a range of baits handy. Peeled prawns, Bass yabbies, squid and pipi are all useful so experiment until you work out what they are feeding on. Flathead respond well to bluebait and squid as do pinkie snapper. Soft plastic grubs are also handy options when the fish aren't responding to bait.

BEST TIDE/TIMES

A tide change around dusk or into the night is best here but make sure you have head lamps as there are no lights in the area. Rough conditions can also be worth a go for bigger snapper.

AMENITIES

There are plenty of amenities in the immediate area such as BBQs, toilets and playground.

KIDS AND FAMILIES

A good location to take the kids as they can run around the park if they're not that into fishing.

FINALLY

An under utilised landbased fishing location that can be very productive for those that spend the time to work it out.

ST HELENS ROCKWALL

HOW TO GET THERE 🔍

Swinburne Street, North Geelong. St Helens Rockwall is located at the end of Swinburne Street which can be reached from Melbourne Road.

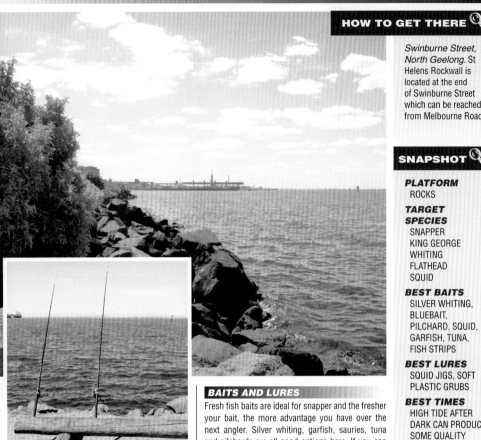

SNAPSHOT 🔍

PLATFORM
ROCKS

TARGET SPECIES
SNAPPER
KING GEORGE WHITING
FLATHEAD
SQUID

BEST BAITS
SILVER WHITING, BLUEBAIT, PILCHARD, SQUID, GARFISH, TUNA, FISH STRIPS

BEST LURES
SQUID JIGS, SOFT PLASTIC GRUBS

BEST TIMES
HIGH TIDE AFTER DARK CAN PRODUCE SOME QUALITY SNAPPER.

This is one of the most popular and productive landbased locations in the Geelong area and for good reason too. Deep water can be accessed with a reasonable cast and there is plenty of space available. It doesn't get more comfortable than here as rods can be set up while anglers wait for them to buckle from the comfort of their cars.

TACTICS

Arrive at least two hours before a high tide and fish until the tide begins to turn back out. Time your visit around dusk and persist after dark during spring and summer for your best shot at big red. Bring a long net or gaff though as landing a big fish can get tricky – particularly after the light fades. Cast artificial squid jigs around weedy areas around dawn and dusk or soft plastics if flathead are on your target list. Lighter surf rods are ideal for King George whiting and your best bet is to cast towards sandy patches between reef.

BAITS AND LURES

Fresh fish baits are ideal for snapper and the fresher your bait, the more advantage you have over the next angler. Silver whiting, garfish, sauries, tuna and pilchards are all good options here. If you can manage a couple of squid from the rockwall they make exceptional baits too. Flathead respond well to half bluebait presentations as well as slowly hopped soft plastics.

BEST TIDE/TIMES

A rising to full tide is perfect for snapper here as they move in to the shallow reef area in search of food. Fish after dark for your best chance at bigger models.

AMENITIES

There are public toilets, a big car park and a playground located nearby.

KIDS AND FAMILIES

A safe location to fish but definitely suited to more serious anglers who are prepared to put the hours in.

FINALLY

A big fish location with plenty of access for a large number of anglers. Spend the hours here and you will reap the rewards.

SEASONS

Snapper
Summer and autumn

King George whiting
Warmer months

Flathead
Summer

Squid
Year round

GRIFFIN GULLY JETTY

🔍 HOW TO GET THERE

The Esplanade, Geelong. Griffins Gully Jetty can be found west of Geelong Waterfront along The Esplanade.

🔍 SNAPSHOT

PLATFORM
JETTY

TARGET SPECIES
AUSTRALIAN SALMON
KING GEORGE WHITING
SNAPPER
SILVER TREVALLY
GARFISH

BEST BAITS
SILVERFISH, MAGGOTS, BLUEBAIT, PILCHARD, BLUEBAIT, SILVER WHITING, SQUID, BASS YABBIES

BEST LURES
SOFT PLASTIC GRUBS AND WORMS, METAL LURES, BLADES

BEST TIMES
HIGH TIDE AS THE AREA BECOMES QUITE SHALLOW AT LOW TIDE.

SEASONS

Australian salmon
Winter and autumn

King George whiting
Summer

Snapper
Summer

Silver trevally
Autumn

Garfish
Summer

This narrow platform provides great fishing during the warmer months and as such receives quite a lot of angler traffic in summer.

TACTICS

Bigger snapper can be fished for with longer surf rods that can send baits out around the moored boats in the area. Use a 20 lb main line and 40 lb leader with a running sinker preferred. Fish into the night if bigger fish are on your agenda here. Garfish can be caught all day and will only require a light rod with 4 lb mono straight through to the hook. Use a pencil float and adjust the depth at which the hooks sit in the water column until you begin to catch a few fish. Silver trevally and salmon schools can turn up from time to time and they respond well to metal lures and soft plastics. The best outfit for these speedsters is a 7 ft graphite stick with a 2500 reel spooled with 6 or 8 lb line.

BAITS AND LURES

Garfish are easily attracted with berley thrown in at constant intervals so be sure to bring plenty with you. Once they are in the area they can be fished for with maggots and silverfish under a pencil float. King George whiting are best targeted with squid and bass yabbies if you can get your hands on some. Australian salmon turn up occasionally and metal lures will do the job while silver trevally respond well to pieces of bluebait and soft plastic creatures. Snapper can be caught on pilchards and whole bluebait.

BEST TIDE/TIMES

A high tide is best here as it does get very shallow when the tide is out. Fish during low light hours for best results.

AMENITIES

There are no amenities in the immediate area but shops and toilets can be located closer to Geelong Waterfront.

KIDS AND FAMILIES

Not a bad location for kids but there isn't a lot of room for them to run around as it is very narrow.

FINALLY

A productive little platform during the warmer months but space can be limited as the best fishing is had along the horizontal section of the pier.

LIMEBURNERS POINT BREAKWALL

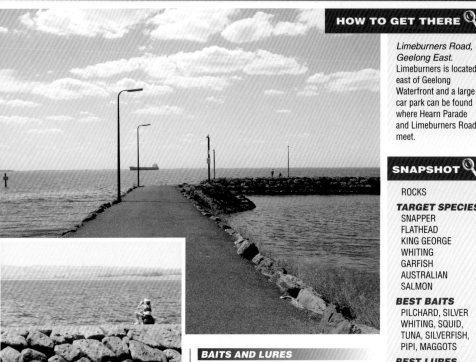

HOW TO GET THERE 🔍

Limeburners Road, Geelong East. Limeburners is located east of Geelong Waterfront and a large car park can be found where Hearn Parade and Limeburners Road meet.

SNAPSHOT 🔍

ROCKS

TARGET SPECIES
SNAPPER
FLATHEAD
KING GEORGE
WHITING
GARFISH
AUSTRALIAN
SALMON

BEST BAITS
PILCHARD, SILVER WHITING, SQUID, TUNA, SILVERFISH, PIPI, MAGGOTS

BEST LURES
METAL LURES, SOFT PLASTIC GRUBS AND WORMS

BEST TIMES
A RISING TIDE DURING DAWN, DUSK OR THROUGHOUT THE NIGHT.

The Limeburners Breakwall was built to provide safe boat launching but has also become a handy fishing platform too. Some big fish can be encountered here for those who are willing to persist well into the night.

TACTICS

Surf rods matched with 4000 to 6000 size reels are ideal for pitching long baits into deeper water for snapper but landing them can be tricky so bring a long net or gaff with you. Snapper can be found in the shallows after dark and usually after or during strong winds. Flathead should be targeted with soft plastics so a 7 to 9 ft rod is ideal. Load 2500 reels with 8 lb braid and 10 lb leaders and fan casts around the length of the breakwall. When schools of Australian salmon can be seen breaking the surface – bring out the metal lures. Garfish can be found in big numbers here but you'll need to attract them to your area with a fine berley mixture of pellets soaked in tuna oil.

BAITS AND LURES

Snapper respond well to whole fish baits such as silver whiting and pilchard but strips of tuna work well here too. King George whiting are a viable target on squid and pipi and garfish are suckers for silverfish. Flathead like a moving bait so hopping soft plastics over the sand patches is a good technique.

BEST TIDE/TIMES

A rising tide is ideal for snapper and King George whiting here whereas an outgoing is best for the local flathead population. Garfish can be caught throughout the entire tide cycle provided enough berley is in the water to keep them interested.

AMENITIES

Large car park and public toilet facilities. The waterfront isn't far away so food and drink supplies can be purchased there before arriving.

KIDS AND FAMILIES

One of the safer breakwalls to fish as a concrete walkway cuts the path between the rocks. Geelong Waterfront is a better option for kids and families though.

FINALLY

A consistent fishery throughout the year with exceptional catches on offer around spring and summer. If you want big fish, persist into the night here.

SEASONS

Snapper
Spring and summer

Flathead
Summer

King George whiting
Summer and autumn

Garfish
Year round

Australian salmon
Winter

CUNNINGHAM PIER

🔍 HOW TO GET THERE

Western Beach, Geelong. Cunningham Pier is located in the heart of Geelong – it really is hard to miss.

🔍 SNAPSHOT

PLATFORM
PIER

TARGET SPECIES
AUSTRALIAN SALMON
SNAPPER
FLATHEAD,
SILVER TREVALLY
GARFISH
KING GEORGE
WHITING
BREAM

BEST BAITS
PILCHARD, SQUID,
BLUEBAIT, SILVER
WHITING, PIPI, BASS
YABBIES

BEST LURES
SOFT PLASTIC
CREATURES AND
WORMS, METAL
LURES

BEST TIMES
TIDE CHANGE AT
DAWN AND DUSK.

SEASONS

Australian salmon
Winter

Snapper
Spring and summer

Flathead
Year round

Silver trevally
Spring

Garfish
Year round

King George whiting
Summer and autumn

Bream
Year round

Cunningham Pier is a large platform that provides anglers with access to deep water along most of its length. A wide variety of species can be caught here and a range of techniques can be implemented. The end of the pier boasts some excellent restaurants too.

TACTICS

Just about every saltwater technique can be implemented here so it pays to have a target in mind, as this will dictate what gear to bring. If you want to target bigger species, a surf rod may be handy as the extra pulling power might be needed. Bring a drop net, gaff or long net though as the drop to the water is a few metres. Garfish can be berleyed up and fished for with a float setup while Australian salmon, trevally, King George whiting and flathead can be fished for with a soft plastic setup, a 2500 reel and 8 lb braid. Bring a variety of jigheads and soft plastics with you as anything can turn up here. A paternoster rig will suffice for most species if you plan to baitfish and sinkers don't need to be overly heavy. Keep in mind – you don't have to cast out far to be in deep water here and species such as bream will often hold tight to the pylons.

BAITS AND LURES

Bream will eat a range of soft plastics, Bass yabbies and prawn while trevally will eat pipi and soft plastic creature baits. Australian salmon can be fished for with metal lures cranked back at high speed and King George whiting will eat squid pipi and Bass yabbies. Snapper prefer larger baits and pilchard, silver whiting and bluebait will get the job done.

BEST TIDE/TIMES

Tide changes are best here with a particular focus on dawn and dusk. Try your luck after dark for a big red.

AMENITIES

Restaurants, toilets, parking and parks in close proximity.

KIDS AND FAMILIES

The pier boasts restaurants and entertainment on weekends so it's perfect for kids and families to spend the day on.

FINALLY

Cunningham Pier offers a variety of fish species to target from a safe, solid structure. There aren't many landbased platforms that drop off into water as deep as here.

GEELONG WATERFRONT

HOW TO GET THERE

Ritchie Boulevard, Geelong. Head along Eastern Beach until you reach the car park on Ritchie Boulevard where parking exists.

SNAPSHOT

PLATFORM
JETTY

TARGET SPECIES
SNAPPER
SILVER TREVALLY
AUSTRALIAN SALMON
BREAM
KING GEORGE
WHITING

BEST BAITS
SQUID, PIPI,
BLUEBAIT, BASS
YABBIES, PILCHARD

BEST LURES
BLADES, SHALLOW
DIVING HARDBODIES,
METAL LURES, SOFT
PLASTIC STICKBAITS
AND CREATURES

BEST TIMES
TIDE CHANGES
AROUND DAWN AND
DUSK.

This picturesque location is very popular with swimmers, walkers and tourists but some goof fishing can be had here throughout the year thanks to access to deep water.

TACTICS

Rods in the 7 ft range are ideal for most of the species here. Spool 2500 size reels up with 6 to 8 lb line and flick plastics, diving hardbodies and blades around the platform for your best chance at flathead bream and silver trevally. The bait anglers can target the same species with light running sinker rigs cast around prominent structure such as the pylons and weed. Use the lightest sinker possible and 6 lb fluorocarbon leaders for your best chance at converting lurkers into takers. Longer casts can be sent out on surf rods for a chance at snapper and bigger baits such as pilchard and silver trevally can be used.

BAITS AND LURES

Blades are ideal here as flathead and bream can't seem to resist them. Slow hop the blades along the bottom and close to the pylons as this is where plenty of bream hang for cover. King George whiting will take squid, pipi and beach worms cast around the weedy areas. When the Australian salmon are about, metal lures and soft plastic stickbaits come into their own. Crank them back with a fast retrieve and they'll chase them down.

BEST TIDE/TIMES

As with most locations, a change of tide is best here. You may only experience a short bite window on the bream so make sure you are here as the tide begins to recede.

AMENITIES

There are plenty of shops and cafes in close proximity. There is a heap of things to see and do on the boardwalk too.

KIDS AND FAMILIES

A top location for kids and families due to the activities available on the boardwalk. The platform is extremely sturdy and contains railing along its length too.

FINALLY

The location can be extremely productive; although, if you like a quiet fish away from the crowds this place may not be ideal as plenty of people walk along its length during summer.

SEASONS

Snapper
Summer and autumn

Silver trevally
Spring

Australian salmon:
Winter

Bream
Year round

King George whiting
Summer & autumn

PORTARLINGTON JETTY

🔍 HOW TO GET THERE

Pier Street, Portarlington. Follow Geelong Road to Portarlington – Pier Street is located at the end of Harding Street.

🔍 SNAPSHOT

PLATFORM
PIER/ROCKS

TARGET SPECIES
GARFISH
SNAPPER
GUMMY SHARKS
AUSTRALIAN SALMON
SQUID
KING GEORGE
 WHITING
SILVER TREVALLY

BEST BAITS
SQUID, SILVER WHITING, SILVERFISH, BLUEBAIT, WHITEBAIT, SALMON, TREVALLY

BEST LURES
METAL LURES, SQUID JIGS, SOFT PLASTICS

BEST TIMES
TIDE CHANGES AROUND DAWN AND DUSK. IF YOU AREN'T FROM THE AREA BUT YOU'RE PLANNING A TRIP, MAKE IT AROUND THE NEW OR FULL MOON.

SEASONS

Garfish
Year round

Snapper
Spring and summer

Gummy sharks
Summer

Australian salmon
Winter

Squid
Year round

King George whiting
Summer and autumn

Silver trevally
Spring

Portarlington Jetty caters to anglers of all skill levels and fish of all sizes can be encountered. Bring a variety of outfits here as you never know what might turn up during the day or night.

TACTICS

With such a wide variety of species on offer it pays to plan your trip in advance. Keep your eye on reports and decide what you want to chase depending on what is available. Surf rods are ideal for chasing snapper with from the top arm of the pier while 7 ft rods are ideal for Australian salmon, trevally and squid. If you plan to chase snapper, make sure you have fresh bait and get here early as spots can be taken pretty quickly when they're in the area. If you just want to kill some time, bring a couple of outfits and two or three different baits. Squid and garfish can be caught in numbers here too so kids will have a ball if they're around.

BAITS AND LURES

Squid jigs will account for good number of the inkers while a silver whiting under a float will do the job too. Snapper will choose a fresh bait over an old one so source the best you can find as competition can be quite high when the reds are in town. Garfish will take silverfish while King George whiting and flathead will take squid.

BEST TIDE/TIMES

Tide changes are best here and an incoming tide is best for most species. If you want to chase snapper, head here after dark three days either side of a new or full moon.

AMENITIES

Good car park, public toilets and a nearby park.

KIDS AND FAMILIES

One of the best landbased locations to take the kids due to the species on offer and available room along the structure. There is also a playground located nearby incase they get bored.

FINALLY

This would have to be one of, if not the best landbased location in Port Phillip Bay mainly because of the space and variety it offers to anglers of all skill level. If you haven't checked it out yet – get on it.

ST LEONARDS PIER

HOW TO GET THERE

The Esplanade,
St Leonards. St
Leonards Pier can be
found at the end of
Murradoc Road along
The Esplanade.

SNAPSHOT

PLATFORM
PIER

TARGET SPECIES
KING GEORGE
WHITING
GARFISH
SNAPPER
FLATHEAD
SQUID
AUSTRALIAN
SALMON

BEST BAITS
SILVER WHITING,
GARFISH, SQUID,
SALMON, PILCHARD,
SILVERFISH

BEST LURES
SOFT PLASTICS,
SQUID JIGS, SABIKI
JIGS

BEST TIMES
DAWN, DUSK AND
INTO THE NIGHT.
FOCUS YOUR
ATTENTION AROUND
A NEW AND FULL
MOON.

S t Leonards Pier can provide some excellent squid fishing during summer and big models are caught every year. The structure is well-built and opens up into some deep water where snapper can be found after strong northerly blows.

TACTICS

A cursory glance into the water will reveal the weed patches that surround the pier – these are the areas you want to cast squid jigs around. Alternatively, and depending on the conditions, you could float a silver whiting under a float around these areas. Snapper arrive in the shallows around spring after a northerly wind has come through so arm yourself with some fresh bait, a surf rod and plenty of patience. Bring a long net or gaff to help you land the big one. Garfish can be tempted close to the structure with a berley bucket filled with pellets, weetbix and tuna oil. Once you've attracted them to the area fish for them with a pencil float rig or sabiki jig. If King George whiting are on your wish list,

cast a paternoster rig with size 6 long shank hooks around the sandy patches between the weed beds.

BAITS AND LURES

Snapper can't pass up fresh bait so do your best to source the freshest bait possible. If you can manage to catch any of the local squid or garfish, send them out on a pair of 5/0 hooks. Squid can be taken on squid jigs or silver whiting and garfish will take small pieces of silverfish on size 12 hooks. King George whiting can be caught with tenderised squid strips and pipi. Casting soft plastics around the sandy shllows will reveal some flathead for those who persist.

BEST TIDE/TIMES

Squid fishing is generally best around dawn and dusk under the lights here. Snapper fishing is particularly good around a new or full moon directly after a strong northerly blow.

AMENITIES

Public toilets and a good car park.

KIDS AND FAMILIES

A good location for the family to spend the day.

FINALLY

A great landbased location for a wide variety of species. If you want to tangle with a landbased snapper, try fishing here during or after a strong northerly blow.

SEASONS

King George whiting
Summer and autumn

Garfish
Summer

Snapper
Spring and summer

Flathead
Warmer months

Squid
Year round

Australian salmon
Winter and spring

SWAN BAY JETTY

HOW TO GET THERE

Swan Bay Road, Swan Bay. Turn down Swan Bay Road from the Bellarine Highway and head to the end before parking in the gravel car park.

SNAPSHOT

PLATFORM
PIER

TARGET SPECIES
GARFISH
GUMMY SHARKS
KING GEORGE
WHITING
MULLET
FLATHEAD

BEST BAITS
SILVERFISH,
MAGGOTS, BLUEBAIT,
SQUID, CURED EEL,
SILVER TREVALLY,
SALMON

BEST LURES
SOFT PLASTICS

BEST TIMES
A HIGH TIDE AFTER
DARK IS MOST
PRODUCTIVE.

SEASONS

Garfish
Year round

Gummy sharks
Year round

King George whiting
Summer and autumn

Mullet
Year round

Flathead
Warmer months

Swan Bay Jetty covers a vast expanse of shallow ground but does drop off towards the final third of the pier. The narrow platform provides the opportunity to tangle with some hefty flathead and gummy sharks during a high tide so it is well worth prospecting.

TACTICS

If you're after gummy sharks, use long surf rods and cast out directly at the end of the pier. Main lines should be in the 20 lb range and attached to leaders of around 40 pound. Use circle hooks in the 5/0 to 7/0 range with decent sized baits attached to them. Both running sinker and paternoster rigs can be used here so use what you are most comfortable with. Allow the rod to fully bend over before setting the hook and make sure your drag is set tight enough for the hook to drive in but not too tight that the fish can't pull any line off without the rod flying in. Garfish are suckers for berley and a good mixture of pellets and tuna oil will bring them into the area when they're in season. Use a pencil float rig with a size 12 hook underneath and you should catch a great feed.

BAITS AND LURES

Gummy sharks are a viable target from the location and they will source out oily baits such as salmon, trevally and cured eel. Flathead will readily take bluebait pieces and squid while garfish prefer small options such as silverfish. You can also flick soft plastics around the end of the pier in search of big flatties.

BEST TIDE/TIMES

The area is relatively shallow so overcast days and night time fishing is best. High tides are also preferred over low tides. Garfish can be caught throughout the day though.

AMENITIES

There are no amenities in the immediate area but a caravan park is located just beyond the gravel car park.

KIDS AND FAMILIES

The platform is extremely narrow so care must be taken at all times. When the garfish are around the kids will have a ball on them. This can be a great way to get the young ones into the sport.

FINALLY

This narrow platform may not look like much but some surprisingly big fish get caught from here each year. Clean water is preferred here so if it's murky you're probably best moving on.

LAKERS CUTTING

HOW TO GET THERE 🔍

Fellows Road, Swan Bay. If you're coming from Geelong, turn left onto Fellows Road from the Bellarine Highway. The fishing are is located approximately 200 m on the right hand side.

SNAPSHOT 🔍

PLATFORM
GRASS/SAND

TARGET SPECIES
BREAM

BEST BAITS
BASS YABBIES, CHICKEN, PRAWN

BEST LURES
SOFT PLASTIC CREATURE BAITS, SHALLOW DIVING HARDBODIES, BLADES

BEST TIMES
FISH AFTER DARK DURING A HIGH TIDE FOR BEST RESULTS.

Leaders should be 4 to 6 lb fluorocarbon but the more experienced would do worse than using 2 lb straight through here. When bait fishing for bream, circle hooks are ideal, as are rod holders that allow rod tips to sit horizontal to the water.

BAITS AND LURES
Bass yabbies are the most productive bait but chicken and peeled prawns also work quite well on the wily bream. Remember though – they don't grow big by being done so stealthy presentations are a must.

BEST TIDE/TIMES
A high tide after dark is best here; however, some cracking bream can be caught during the day when skies are overcast.

AMENITIES
There are no amenities in the immediate area.

KIDS AND FAMILIES
Not the best location for smaller children but keen young anglers might enjoy the serenity of the place at night.

FINALLY
While the area may look a little uninspiring, the fish that live here certainly throw that idea out the window.

SEASONS
Bream
Year round

Lakers Cutting is one of the less-likely looking fishing areas in the region but if bream are high on your wish list – this place produces some crackers, particularly at night. The area is quite shallow so low light conditions are best here.

TACTICS
Light rods, lines and presentations are all required to fool the wily bream that frequently inhabit the area. Bait fishing is popular here and lightly weighted (or unweighted) Bass yabbies are the best presentation to use. For the lure anglers, casting soft plastic creature baits is effective so long as you impart a slow retrieve. Suitable rods include 7 ft graphite varieties as well as quiver tips.

QUEENSCLIFF PIER

HOW TO GET THERE

Symonds Street, Queenscliff. Follow the Bellarine Highway into Queenscliff before turning down Symonds Street.

SNAPSHOT

PLATFORM
PIER

TARGET SPECIES
SQUID
GARFISH
KING GEORGE
WHITING
SILVER TREVALLY

BEST BAITS
SQUID, PIPI,
SILVERFISH, SILVER
WHITING, GARFISH,
PILCHARD

BEST LURES
SOFT PLASTIC
CREATURE BAITS,
SQUID JIGS

BEST TIMES
DAWN AND DUSK
AROUND A CHANGE
OF TIDE.

SEASONS

Squid
Year round

Garfish
Year round

King George whiting
Summer

Silver trevally
Spring and summer

Queenscliff Pier is fantastic for a range of species but squid are high on the agenda of most anglers here. The pier is well constructed, features plenty of room and boasts a sheltered area for when the weather gets nasty. It does get busy here when squid are in the area but it is worth persisting with as big numbers can be caught around dawn and dusk.

TACTICS

A paternoster rig is great for targeting whiting and flathead on and long shank hooks are best. Red tubing placed above hooks will also help to attract whiting. Use as much weight as needed to anchor the bait close to the bottom without going too heavy. Squid jigs should be cast around the weedy patches and if you're in doubt of where they are just look for the squid ink on the pier. Garfish can be attracted with plenty of berley and a berley bucket left to waft around in the water will be beneficial to keeping fish in the area. Light rods in the 2 to 4 kg range and 7 ft in length will get the job done here.

BAITS AND LURES

Artificial squid jigs in the 3.0 size are best for the local squid population; however, a silver whiting under a float will also take its fair share of fish. Soft plastics will account for flathead and silver trevally when they are in the area. King George whiting are suckers for a squid and pipi cocktail bait.

BEST TIDE/TIMES

Incoming and outgoing tides are best for all of the species here but pay particular attention to dusk and into the night for squid. Garfish can be caught throughout the day as can King George whiting.

AMENITIES

There is a good car park available as well as public toilets. The pier itself also features a large covered area for inclement weather.

KIDS AND FAMILIES

A great location to take the kids thanks to a sturdy platform and adjacent beach for them to play on when the fishing is slow.

FINALLY

One of the most consistent squid fishing platforms in Port Phillip Bay.

THE CUT – QUEENSCLIFF

○ GET THERE

Larkin Parade, Queenscliff. Follow Wharf Street until it turns into Larkin Parade. The Cut is located behind the buildings at Queenscliff Harbour.

SNAPSHOT

PLATFORM
PIER

TARGET SPECIES
SILVER TREVALLY
BREAM
AUSTRALIAN SALMON
TOMMY ROUGH
SQUID
FLATHEAD
GARFISH
KING GEORGE WHITING

BEST BAITS
PIPI, SQUID, PILCHARD, SILVERFISH, BASS YABBIES, BLUEBAIT

BEST LURES
SOFT PLASTIC WORMS, STICKBAITS, CREATURES AND GRUBS

BEST TIMES
AS THE TIDE RIPS THROUGH HERE DURING A TIDE CHANGE, SLACK WATER IS THE BEST OPTION.

SEASONS

Silver trevally
Spring and summer

Bream
Year round

Australian salmon
Autumn

Squid
Summer

Flathead
Warmer months

Garfish
Summer

King George whiting
Summer

This popular section of water cuts through the north of the peninsula and connects Swan bay to Port Phillip bay. The tide rips through the narrow pathway so fishing can be tough here at times. Thankfully, plenty of fish swim through the area and landbased anglers can get amongst it from one of the local jetties. Big silver trevally draw large numbers of anglers here each year and for good reason too – they provide great sport, taste pretty good and make excellent shark bait.

TACTICS

Plan your trip here around slack water either side of a high or low tide. Soft plastics are the best option for the silver trevally here but bring a range of jigheads along to work out how much weight is needed to get into the strikezone. If the silver trevally are schooling up in the area you'll know about it as the place will be busy. Keep an eye on what the locals are doing and then mimic them as they have the place pretty sussed out. Bait fishing is

a simple affair here and paternoster rigs will suffice. Sinkers will probably need to be heavier than you would normally use so bring a variety with you. Leader material should be in the 6 to 8 lb range when flicking soft plastics around and 2 to 4 kg rods in the 6 to 7 ft range will do the job nicely.

BAITS AND LURES

A wide variety of bait can be used here but soft plastics tend to work best on most species. Silver trevally love worm style soft plastics while Australian salmon prefer stickbait profiles. Garfish can be taken on silverfish under a float while squid are best fished for at night with squid jigs. Bream can be targeted around the pylons with blades and Bass yabbies.

BEST TIDE/TIMES

The two to three hours in between tides is best here as the slack water is a lot easier to fish – especially for the inexperienced.

AMENITIES

There are some shops and public toilets located at Queenscliff Harbour.

KIDS AND FAMILIES

Kids will need to be supervised at all times as the current is strong through here.

FINALLY

A hard area to fish due to the raging tide but some pretty excellent rewards are on offer for those that know how to fish it. Follow what the locals are doing for best results.

POINT LONSDALE PIER

🔍 HOW TO GET THERE

Point Lonsdale Road, Point Lonsdale. Follow the Bellarine Highway until you reach Point Lonsdale Road. Park in the gravel car park at the end of the road.

🔍 SNAPSHOT

PLATFORM
PIER

TARGET SPECIES
SHARKS
KING GEORGE WHITING
KINGFISH
SNAPPER
SQUID
GARFISH
AUSTRALIAN SALMON

BEST BAITS
TUNA, SALMON, TREVALLY, PILCHARD, BLUEBAIT, SQUID, PIPI, SILVERFISH

BEST LURES
SURFACE POPPERS, METAL LURES, SQUID JIGS, SOFT PLASTIC GRUBS AND STICKBAITS

BEST TIMES
TIDE CHANGES AROUND DAWN AND DUSK.

SEASONS

Sharks
All year but summer is best

King George whiting
Summer

Kingfish
Summer

Snapper
Spring

Squid
Year round

Garfish
Year round

Australian salmon
Winter

Point Lonsdale Pier is one of the most exciting landbased platforms in Port Phillip Bay due to its close proximity to The Rip. A wide variety of species can be caught here (basically all that swim in the port) and as such a wide variety of techniques can be implemented. Big sharks are a prized-catch here and some truly big monsters have been caught here over the years.

TACTICS

With such a vast array of species on offer it pays to have a target species in mind before embarking on a session here. By selecting a target species, anglers will have a better idea of what tackle to bring. Overhead game rods are best suited for bigger sharks while surf rods are well suited to pitching baits for salmon, snapper, King George whiting and smaller sharks. A big bait sitting under a balloon is ideal for big sharks and heavy wire traces are a must. Do plenty of research on landbased game techniques for your best chance. Squid jigs cast around the weedy areas will attract the resident cephalopods but remember to bring a long net or squid gaff for your best chance to land the bigger guys. During kingfish season it pays to cast big surface lures around the end of the pier but good luck landing them around the reefy bottom.

BAITS AND LURES

Big baits such as salmon, tuna and trevally are ideal for sharks while snapper are best targeted with pilchards, silver whiting and fresh squid. Garfish respond well to silverfish floated under a pencil float and King George whiting can't resist a cocktail bait of squid and pipi. When Australian salmon are in the area, metal lures are the go.

BEST TIDE/TIMES

Tide changes around dawn and dusk make for the best time to chase the majority of species but if

it's big sharks you're after, stay on after dark. Be prepared to put in a lot of hours though.

AMENITIES

There is public toilet facilities and a car park situated on the foreshore.

KIDS AND FAMILIES

While the pier is very productive, it is built high above the water level so children need to be supervised at all times. The beach provides a good area for kids and families to spend the day on.

FINALLY

Point Lonsdale pier is the best landbased location in the port to encounter big fish on a regular basis.

FISHING KNOTS

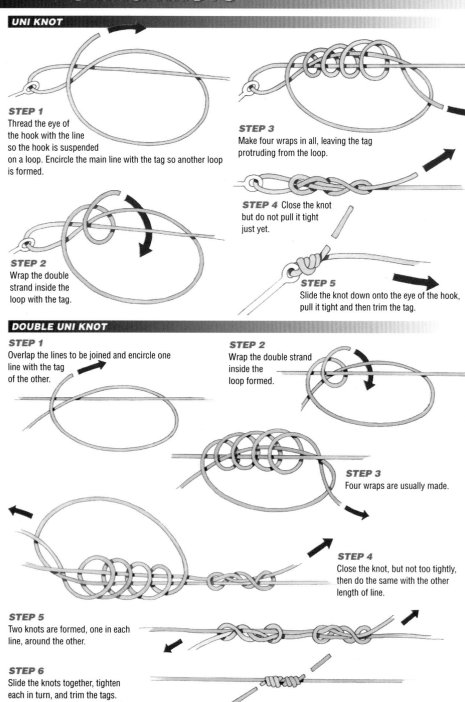

STEP 1
Thread the eye of
the hook with the line
so the hook is suspended
on a loop. Encircle the main line with the tag so another loop
is formed.

STEP 2
Wrap the double
strand inside the
loop with the tag.

STEP 3
Make four wraps in all, leaving the tag
protruding from the loop.

STEP 4 Close the knot
but do not pull it tight
just yet.

STEP 5
Slide the knot down onto the eye of the hook,
pull it tight and then trim the tag.

DOUBLE UNI KNOT

STEP 1
Overlap the lines to be joined and encircle one
line with the tag
of the other.

STEP 2
Wrap the double strand
inside the
loop formed.

STEP 3
Four wraps are usually made.

STEP 4
Close the knot, but not too tightly,
then do the same with the other
length of line.

STEP 5
Two knots are formed, one in each
line, around the other.

STEP 6
Slide the knots together, tighten
each in turn, and trim the tags.

LOCKED BLOOD KNOT

STEP 1
Thread the eye of your hook or swivel and
twist the tag and main line together.

STEP 2
Complete three to six
twists and thread the tag back
through the first twist. The heavier your line,
the less twists you will use.

STEP 3
Pull the line so that the knot begins to form,
but not up tight yet as it will make an unlocked
half blood which may slip. Lock the knot by threading the tag
through the open loop that has formed at the top of the knot.

STEP 4
Pull the knot up firmly. Should a loop form within
the knot, simply pull on the tag until it disappears.

COMMON SNELL

STEP 1
Make the
configuration
shown.

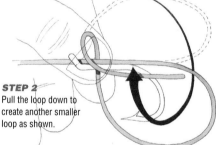

STEP 2
Pull the loop down to
create another smaller
loop as shown.

STEP 3
Keep wrapping the
shank of the hook and
the tag.

STEP 4
Keep wrapping until the
desired number of wraps
are in place.

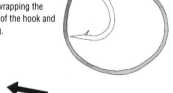

STEP 5
Pull the main line and
the tag until the knot is
formed.

STEP 5
It is preferred that the snell is formed down a little
from the eye so chances of separation by a roughly
turned or sharp eye are reduced. Trim the tag.

FISHING KNOTS

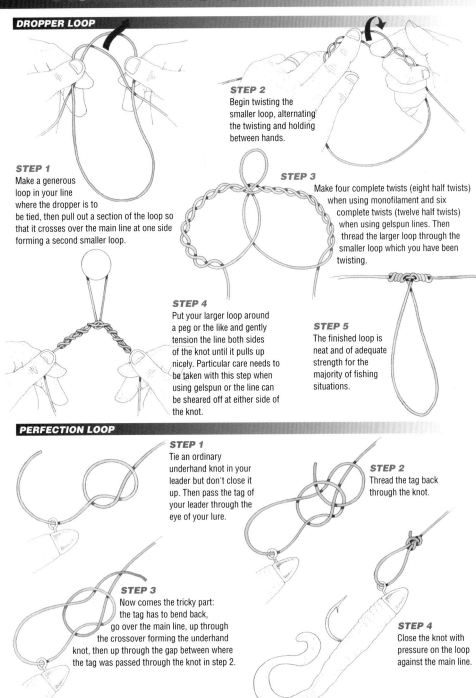

DROPPER LOOP

STEP 1
Make a generous loop in your line where the dropper is to be tied, then pull out a section of the loop so that it crosses over the main line at one side forming a second smaller loop.

STEP 2
Begin twisting the smaller loop, alternating the twisting and holding between hands.

STEP 3
Make four complete twists (eight half twists) when using monofilament and six complete twists (twelve half twists) when using gelspun lines. Then thread the larger loop through the smaller loop which you have been twisting.

STEP 4
Put your larger loop around a peg or the like and gently tension the line both sides of the knot until it pulls up nicely. Particular care needs to be taken with this step when using gelspun or the line can be sheared off at either side of the knot.

STEP 5
The finished loop is neat and of adequate strength for the majority of fishing situations.

PERFECTION LOOP

STEP 1
Tie an ordinary underhand knot in your leader but don't close it up. Then pass the tag of your leader through the eye of your lure.

STEP 2
Thread the tag back through the knot.

STEP 3
Now comes the tricky part: the tag has to bend back, go over the main line, up through the crossover forming the underhand knot, then up through the gap between where the tag was passed through the knot in step 2.

STEP 4
Close the knot with pressure on the loop against the main line.

RUNNING SINKER RIG

A running sinker rig is one of the most versatile rigs that can be used for Western Port or where an area is affected by fast current. Locations such as Stony Point pier require the use of this style of rig. This rig is mainly used when targeting gummy sharks, elephant fish and snapper.

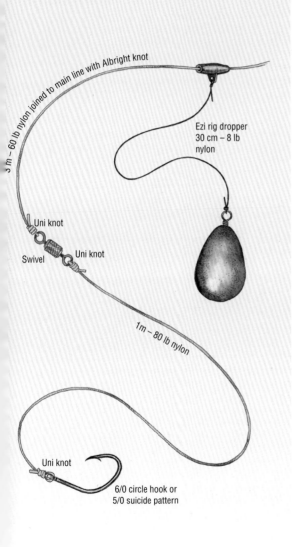

3 m – 60 lb nylon joined to main line with Albright knot

Ezi rig dropper
30 cm – 8 lb nylon

Uni knot

Swivel

Uni knot

1m – 80 lb nylon

Uni knot

6/0 circle hook or
5/0 suicide pattern

GARFISH FLOAT RIG

Garfish are a top water feeder, meaning they swim and feed just under the water's surface. When targeting them, a float setup will allow a bait to be suspended in their feeding zone. The float will also act as a bite indicator for anglers to see when the bait has been taken and the fish is hooked.

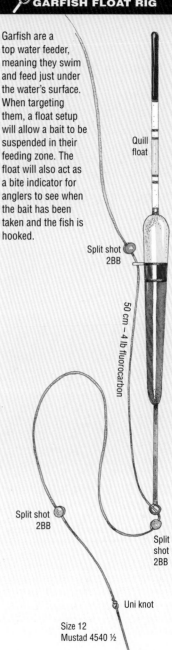

Quill float

Split shot 2BB

50 cm – 4 lb fluorocarbon

Split shot 2BB

Split shot 2BB

Uni knot

Size 12
Mustad 4540 ½

GUMMY SHARK RIG

SQUID FLOAT RIG

Landbased anglers fishing for calamari don't always get the casting distance required when using an artificial jig. The baited float rig is highly effective and allows the bait to be suspended by the float to hover just above the weed beds. The float will need to be set according to the depth fished, and when right works exceptionally well.

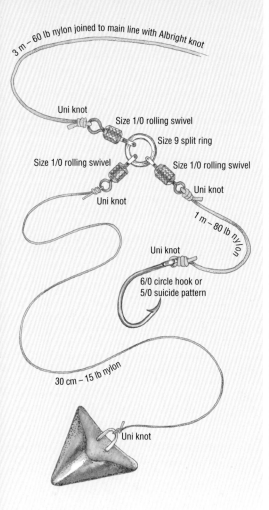

3 m – 60 lb nylon joined to main line with Albright knot

Uni knot

Size 1/0 rolling swivel

Size 9 split ring

Size 1/0 rolling swivel

Size 1/0 rolling swivel

Uni knot

Uni knot

1 m – 80 lb nylon

Uni knot

6/0 circle hook or 5/0 suicide pattern

30 cm – 15 lb nylon

Uni knot

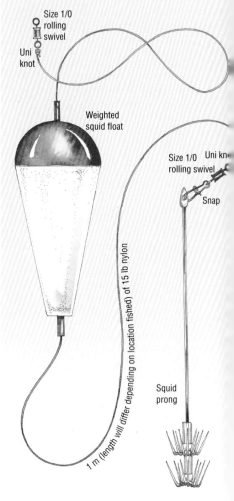

Size 1/0 rolling swivel

Uni knot

Weighted squid float

Size 1/0 rolling swivel

Uni knot

Snap

1 m (length will differ depending on location fished) of 15 lb nylon

Squid prong

The gummy shark rig is mainly used in surf fishing situations. This rig has been manipulated to allow the sinker to sit in the sand without needing too much drag pressure bestowed on the reel as with a running sinker rig. The use of the swivel and split rig setup is to prevent line twist in a strong swell or side wash situation. Strictly used for gummy shark, it is a highly recommended rig to use

LANDBASED FISHING RIGS

WHITING PATERNOSTER RIG

Size 1/0
rolling
swivel

Uni knot

opper loop

Uni knot

Size 1/0 circle
or size 6 long
shank

50 cm – 15 lb flurocarbon

Uni knot

Dropper loop

ize 1/0 circle
r size 6 long
hank

Uni knot

A paternoster rig is one of the most commonly used rigs in fishing but there are plenty of variations about. The whiting version is made to allow the baits to sit just above the weed beds. Designed to be used with circle hooks, this rig is perfect when fishing in fast current situations. Not only good for whiting but this rig will also catch trevally, flathead and salmon.

SALMON PATERNOSTER RIG

Another variation of the paternoster rig, the salmon paternoster is made from a little heavier tackle than the whiting. This rig is ideal for surf fishing as it allows two baits to be suspended in the water column. This rig is strictly used for surf fishing and is ideal for salmon.

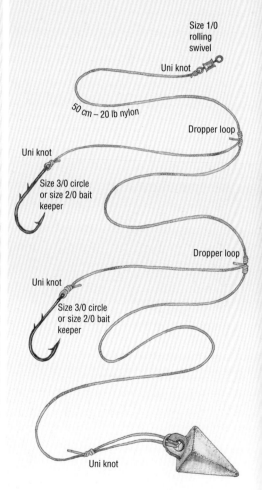

Size 1/0
rolling
swivel

Uni knot

50 cm – 20 lb nylon

Dropper loop

Uni knot

Size 3/0 circle
or size 2/0 bait
keeper

Dropper loop

Uni knot

Size 3/0 circle
or size 2/0 bait
keeper

Uni knot

BAIT PRESENTATION

CALAMARI RING

A calamari ring bait is one of the most effective and simplest ways to fish with calamari for bait. Rings are mainly used when fishing in fast current situations so as to prevent the bait from spinning in the current. Once pinned on the hooks, the ring will sit in the current and slowly sway with the pressure of the water. This bait presentation is perfect for snapper, elephant fish, gummy shark and mulloway.

FILLET BAIT

Fillets are fantastic to use if fresh. They are easy to cut from a whole fish and can be pinned using two hooks. In fast tidal areas, fillet baits may spin, causing line twist and put off fish from taking it. They are best used at locations such as Stockyard Point or Lang Lang.
This bait presentation is most effective on snapper and gummy sharks.

FISH HEAD

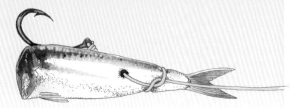

Whole fish heads are used when targeting big fish. Heads should be cut from the pectoral fin and pinned using one hook through the mouth region. Head baits can be used in any location and sit well when used with a single hook. Fish heads are suitable for gummy sharks, snapper and toothy sharks.

HALF PILCHARD

A half pilchard is a neat little bait that can be used for a variety of species. The bait itself should be cut in half and pinned using a single hook with a half hitch around the tail section to keep it straight. Baiting this way is ideal when fishing the surf for salmon.

BAIT PRESENTATION

When fishing for whiting, pipi baits are the most popular bait used. When placing on the hook, it is imperative that they be neatly pinned, then wrapped and re-pinned on the hook. This prevents them from being taken off the hook. Perfect for whiting, salmon and silver trevally.

SQUID STRIP

Often, big baits can deter fish which is where a small strip of squid is ideal. Using either a tentacle or straight piece of calamari hood, the squid strip can be pinned on either a single hook or two hook setup. Squid strips are ideal for targeting snapper, gummy sharks and elephant fish.

WHOLE BLUEBAIT OR PILCHARD

Bluebait or pilchards can also be fished whole and are recommended for big salmon. This bait is recommended for salmon in the surf or snapper and flathead in calmer water. If not pinned on the hooks correctly, they can spin in the current. They can be used with either a single hook rig or twin hook rig. Either way, they will require a half hitch on the tail to keep inline.

WHOLE FISH

When fishing for snapper a whole bait is recommended. This bait, regardless of type of fish used, must be rigged using two hooks to hold straight and to prevent from falling off the hook. One hook should be placed in the head while the other in the tail section with a half hitch around the tail. This presentation is ideal for all snapper situations.

TARGET FISH ID GUIDE

AUSTRALIAN SALMON

BAG LIMIT
20

MINIMUM LENGTH
21 cm

GROWS TO
90 cm / 9 kg

BARRACOUTA

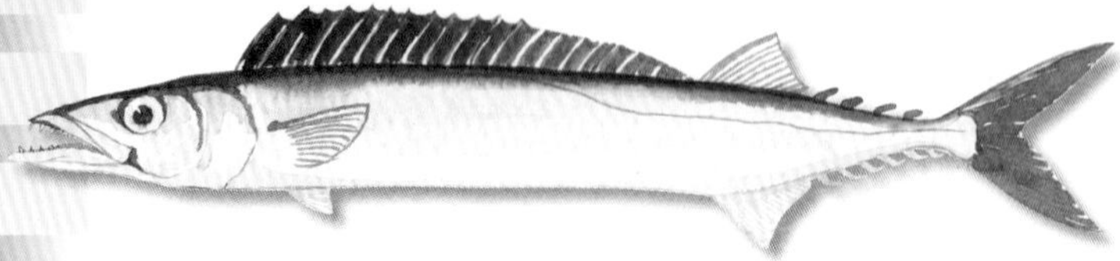

BAG LIMIT
20

MINIMUM LENGTH
No size limit

GROWS TO
130 cm / 5 kg

BLUE MORWONG

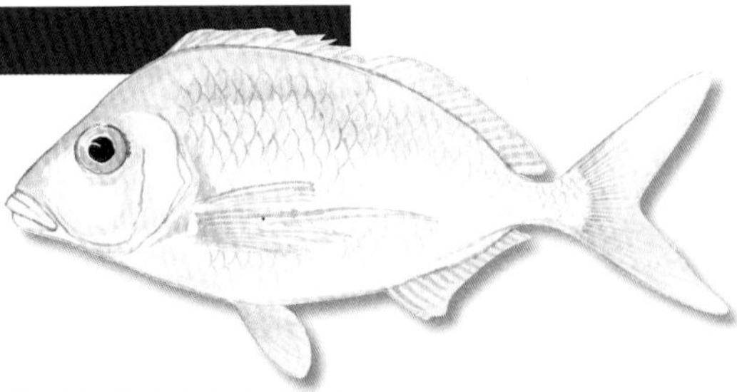

BAG LIMIT
5

MINIMUM LENGTH
23 cm

GROWS TO
140 cm / 40 kg

BLUE THROATED WRASSE

BAG LIMIT
5 *Total of one species or more*

MINIMUM LENGTH
27 cm

GROWS TO
40 cm / 1 kg

BREAM FAMILY

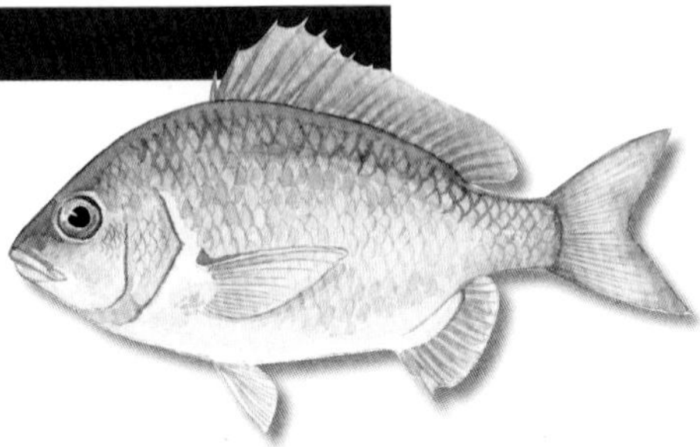

BAG LIMIT
10

MINIMUM LENGTH
28 cm

GROWS TO
60 cm / 3.5 kg

TARGET FISH ID GUIDE

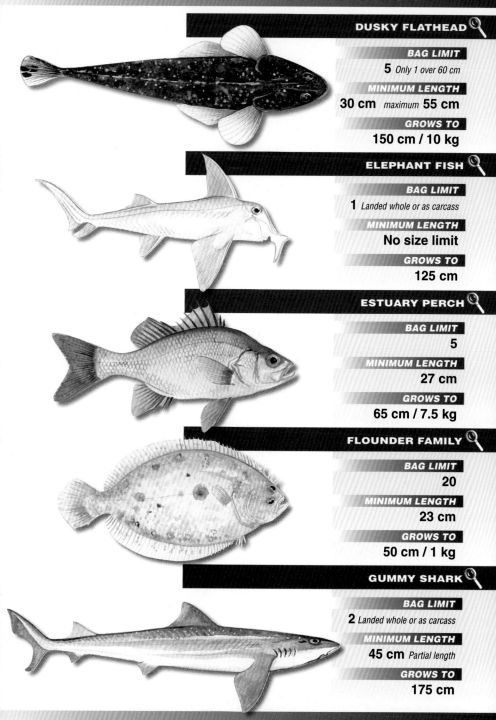

DUSKY FLATHEAD

BAG LIMIT
5 *Only 1 over 60 cm*

MINIMUM LENGTH
30 cm *maximum* 55 cm

GROWS TO
150 cm / 10 kg

ELEPHANT FISH

BAG LIMIT
1 *Landed whole or as carcass*

MINIMUM LENGTH
No size limit

GROWS TO
125 cm

ESTUARY PERCH

BAG LIMIT
5

MINIMUM LENGTH
27 cm

GROWS TO
65 cm / 7.5 kg

FLOUNDER FAMILY

BAG LIMIT
20

MINIMUM LENGTH
23 cm

GROWS TO
50 cm / 1 kg

GUMMY SHARK

BAG LIMIT
2 *Landed whole or as carcass*

MINIMUM LENGTH
45 cm *Partial length*

GROWS TO
175 cm

KING GEORGE WHITING

BAG LIMIT
20 *Landed whole or as carcass*

MINIMUM LENGTH
27 cm

GROWS TO
67 cm / 2 kg

LEATHERJACKET FAMILY

BAG LIMIT
20

MINIMUM LENGTH
No size limit

GROWS TO
60 cm

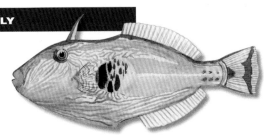

LING FAMILY

BAG LIMIT
5

MINIMUM LENGTH
30 cm

GROWS TO
110 cm / 8 kg

MULLET FAMILY

BAG LIMIT
40

MINIMUM LENGTH
No size limit

GROWS TO
80 cm / 5 kg

MULLOWAY

BAG LIMIT
5

MINIMUM LENGTH
60 cm

GROWS TO
180 cm / 60 kg

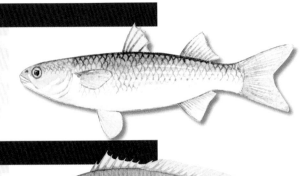

TARGET FISH ID GUIDE

SILVER TREVALLY

BAG LIMIT
20

MINIMUM LENGTH
20 cm

GROWS TO
100 cm / 11 kg

SNAPPER

BAG LIMIT
10

MINIMUM LENGTH
28 cm *no more than 3 greater than or equal to 40 cm*

GROWS TO
125 cm / 19 kg

SOUTHERN BLUE SPOT FLATHEAD

BAG LIMIT
20

MINIMUM LENGTH
27 cm

GROWS TO
100 cm / 8 kg

SQUID, OCTOPUS, CUTTLEFISH

BAG LIMIT
10 *Total for one or more species*

MINIMUM LENGTH
No size limit

GROWS TO
Varies between species

TAILOR

BAG LIMIT
20

MINIMUM LENGTH
23 cm

GROWS TO
120 cm / 17 kg

TARGET FISH ID GUIDE

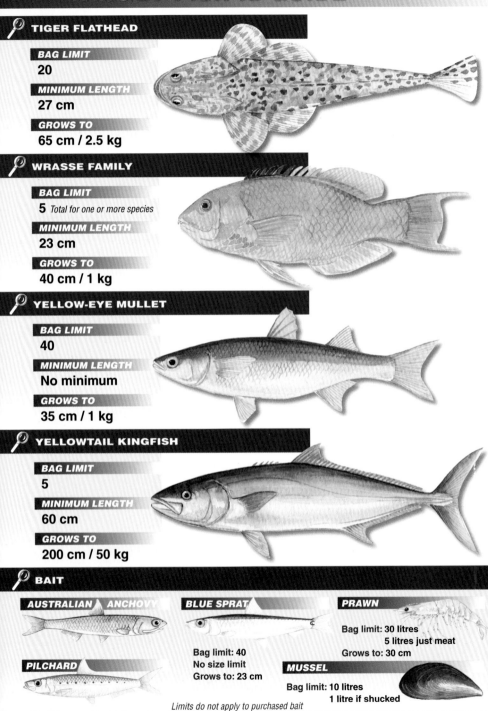

TIGER FLATHEAD

BAG LIMIT
20

MINIMUM LENGTH
27 cm

GROWS TO
65 cm / 2.5 kg

WRASSE FAMILY

BAG LIMIT
5 *Total for one or more species*

MINIMUM LENGTH
23 cm

GROWS TO
40 cm / 1 kg

YELLOW-EYE MULLET

BAG LIMIT
40

MINIMUM LENGTH
No minimum

GROWS TO
35 cm / 1 kg

YELLOWTAIL KINGFISH

BAG LIMIT
5

MINIMUM LENGTH
60 cm

GROWS TO
200 cm / 50 kg

BAIT

AUSTRALIAN ANCHOVY

BLUE SPRAT

Bag limit: 40
No size limit
Grows to: 23 cm

PRAWN

Bag limit: 30 litres
         5 litres just meat
Grows to: 30 cm

PILCHARD

MUSSEL

Bag limit: 10 litres
1 litre if shucked

Limits do not apply to purchased bait

Victorian Fisheries AUTHORITY

The freshest fish without the mess!

Taking home fresh seafood has never been easier with new fish cleaning tables around the state, thanks to the State Government's $35 million *Target One Million* Plan to get more people fishing, more often in more places.

The Warmies is one of the locations to score a new facility. It's a popular spot for land-based fishers near Williamstown and gives great access to a range of species including bream, flathead and tailor.

The new table means it's easier than ever for you to take home the very freshest fish for your family and friends to enjoy.

It's under cover, connected to running water and boasts lighting so it can be used 24/7.

It's one of several new fish cleaning tables being constructed across Victoria thanks to *Target One Million*.

Target One Million
More Victorians fishing, more often